宋官窯特展圖錄

# 宋官窯特展

# Catalogue of the Special Exhibition
# of Sung Dynasty Kuan Ware

國立故宮博物院
National Palace Museum

# 目　錄

# Contents

# 宋官窯特展說明

蔡和璧

　　此次宋官窯特展共選件展出壹佰四十三件，全部沿用故宮博物院原典藏名稱——北宋官窯、南宋脩內司官窯，南宋郊壇下官窯——三個名稱展示。

　　本院所藏之宋官窯不論在質與量方面都相當豐富，以次展出特別精美者，如展品67、68號葵花式盌，薄胎薄釉，葵口線條柔美。展品58號粉青葵花式洗，其用途爲調整筆墨之濃淡，葵花瓣之稜線明顯，層次分明，亦屬薄胎薄釉，胎土褐黑自然，起稜處稍呈紫，但流釉處所呈紫色並不很明顯，爲難得之精品。展品8號粉青貫耳弦紋壺，高爲38.2公分，爲現今所知道的最大一件，由於大件胎略厚一些，雙貫耳比例相當大，與豐滿的圓腹相配非常調和大方。而展品80、81、82、83、88、90號皆爲圓洗，其器底有六支釘燒者，亦有墊圈燒者，釉之透明度與厚度皆較上述之67、68、58號爲厚，器型端莊、柔和。展品9、10號爲貫耳弦紋壺、器型穩重大方、釉開片自然，片紋呈自然無染色，積釉處呈冰裂。口緣釉稍流呈現淡紫色。展品2號粉青尊，以整體造型而言口緣略顯拘謹，可能由於原收藏時喇叭口緣微有損，故磨去一圈後覆上銅口。此件造形典雅，釉厚滋潤，釉積處呈碧湖綠，非常秀麗。展品35號簋式爐之釉色可與2號尊相媲美，或更甚之，令人覺得深奧無比。爐之雙象耳，在耳下可能因燒造時垂釉的關係，被磨而露出黑紫色胎，製做謹飭，爐足圓形而爐口呈橢圓形，更顯出純熟的製作技巧。展品44號長方盆亦可稱大件，雖然胎厚，釉亦厚，釉色與上述之2號35號一樣典美，且呈多層次的冰裂。另外盤盌類如展品98、99、100、101、102號皆屬上乘之作。器型多屬折腰花口，非常秀氣，而盌類則展品103、106、107號器型口腹圓、可與盤等類搭配調和。此次特展中，92號菱花式盤、93號蓮花式盤、94號牡丹花式盤、95號菊花式盤，皆爲花式盤，造型秀麗典雅，可謂花形器皿中最精緻者。

本院之宋、元瓷器大都在清前三朝時收入宮內，因此這些宋官窯由外而收入宮內。在康熙十六年時，紅樓夢作者，曹雪芹之曾祖曹璽留有一貢品單，內記貢書畫、瓷器及珍玩物品之名稱與件數，這顯示清朝皇帝自入關接繼明皇室紫禁域畿，政治在逐漸安定下來後，對於歷代所遺留之名畫名品逐漸產生興趣，並加以收集，尤其是乾隆帝，更是由於國盛富强，藝術修養豐富，故在乾隆朝時，名畫名品被收入宮中最多。除了宋朝所作的官窯外宋龍泉所燒之仿官及元、明各朝的仿官之作亦因進貢者所識有限皆雜而入宮內，此次名爲宋官窯特展，除了展出極精美之宋官窯外，另擇元、明、清及宋龍泉所仿之精品同時展出，以資對宋官窯及官釉作品之系統做整體的瞭解與比較。本文亦對官窯之名稱稍做詮釋。並試對歷代文獻記載之情況加以討論，以期對宋官窯更有明確的瞭解。

「官窯」可做廣義與狹意的區分，即普通名詞及專有名詞之分，前者泛指承官命燒造以供宮廷使用者，在文獻中如禮記曲禮便有「天子之六工曰土工，金工，石工，木工，獸工，草工，典制六材」。陶之工曰土工。這些皆是官工，又在唐六典中有「將作監，甄官署令一人，從八品下」。舊唐書·職官志「甄官署令一人，丞二人，府五人，吏十人，監作四人，典事十八人，掌供琢石陶土之事……」。以上略舉之資料爲官屬之工匠，其職掌專爲宮廷燒造相關事宜之器物。另外以其地方之土產貢於宮廷者，雖非官府指定，但必定是方物名產並檢其精良者才入貢，如唐六典卷三「河北道貢邢州瓷器」，是一例。宋初，吳越錢氏屢屢向王室貢瓷是二例，宋朝王存「元豐九域志」卷三記「耀州華原郡上貢瓷器五十事。」是三例。一旦將土產精品入貢於宮廷，在意義上便可稱爲官窯。以上列舉皆可稱之爲廣義的官窯，它包括官屬工匠所製作的或非一般流通性之商品，當然這其中包括有經常性與特殊性的，即是「有命則貢，無命則止」的情況。降至明、清，在景德鎮設置御窯廠，派遣專人管理，燒造宮廷器皿，特別是自康熙二十年由內府遣官，發內帑支銷其用度，官窯的特殊性更爲明顯。到了乾隆後期，景德鎮之御窯廠改由浮梁縣知巡檢管理直到清末。對於官窯的觀念漸衍成如「匋雅」所言「 官窯之尤精者命曰御窯，御窯也者，至尊之所御也。官窯者，妃嬪以下所得用也 」。時至民國初，「飲流齋説瓷」中稱「 清代於官窯之中更有御窯，專備御用而不敢僭，若官窯者則貴人達官亦得用之 」。由前引的歷代文獻記載可以約略看出廣意官窯的疇範。

至於屬於專有名詞的官窯則是指宋朝五大名窯—— 定、汝、官、哥、鈞—— 中的官窯。關於官窯最早的記載爲「説郛」所錄南宋末顧文薦的「負喧雜錄」及「輟耕錄」載葉寘的「坦齋筆衡」二則資料。這兩則記載在文字上近乎相同。由於葉寘爲何時人已不可考，故不知何者爲先何者後。今舉顧文薦所記：「 本朝以定州白瓷器有芒不堪用，遂命汝州造青窯器，故河北唐、鄧、耀州悉有之，汝窯爲魁，江南則處州龍泉縣窯質頗麤厚。宣政間，京師自置窯燒造，名曰官窯。中興渡江，有邵成章提舉後苑，號邵局，襲故京遺制，置窯于修內司，造青器，名內窯，澄泥爲範，極其精緻。油色瑩澈，爲世所珍。後郊下別立新窯，亦曰官窯，比舊窯大不侔矣。餘如烏泥窯，餘姚窯，續窯，皆非官窯比。若謂舊越窯，不復見矣 」。這個記載也是宋時人記載當代官窯的資料，質而言之，可分北宋官窯，南宋脩內司官窯，南宋郊壇下官窯。此則記載自南宋直到清乾隆爲止的六百年間，却找不到徵引其文者。直到清後期顧文薦的這則資料才爲人重視。宋官窯之三分法—— 北宋官窯，南宋脩內司官窯，南宋郊壇下官窯於是沿用至今。然而由於近年考古工作的積極進行，發掘層面擴大，唐宋以來的名窯窯址接二連三地發現與調查，如河南寶豐縣清凉寺址的汝窯窯址及杭州郊壇下附近南宋官窯窯址等已進行挖掘整理，這些在在對中國陶瓷史而言佔有重要的一頁。由於本院所藏之宋官窯大部份皆在清前期收入宮中，距宋朝有六、七百年，其間對官窯認知的差距，各方搜羅進貢入宮的標準不一，再加上清朝之仿製盛行，造成今人對宋官窯看法的分歧。

　　本文試將歷代記載官窯資料稍作介紹與分析，並就本院藏品加以檢討，以期瞭解歷代對宋官窯的認識。首先就顧氏將官窯作三分法中所提及的北宋官窯來作檢討。在乾隆以後陶書的記載皆根據顧文薦所言「宣政間，京師自置窯燒造，名曰官窯」從而認爲北宋除了汝窯，應另有北宋官窯。據此，北宋官窯理應置窯於京，換而言之窯址當在開封附近，其產品之器胎、釉質應屬河南系統。但就本院收藏的一批原典藏品名爲北宋官窯之實物而觀察，釉質皆屬半失透，氣泡少。釉層各有厚薄不同，釉色有天藍、天青、灰青、月白。器口緣及圈足的處理技法亦多歧異。器胎土有灰白、灰黑、褐黑等非河南系之胎土。仔細觀察，其共同點僅在於半失透釉，氣泡少而已。有些作品甚至將釉表加工研磨，使釉面光消失達到半失透釉的效果。因爲開封一帶歷代有過幾次大水災，並由於黃土淤泥覆掩層厚，考古發掘工作至今仍無法著手進行，開封附近是否有北宋官窯窯址，若是有產品是否與本院所藏這批相類，目前皆無從知曉。

　　在文獻資料中尚有宋代「宣和奉使高麗圖經」一書略有關於陶瓷的記載，但並沒有提及北宋官窯，只言及定窯，越州窯、汝州新窯器。在器皿項下記述一些器物的形制，以「陶爐」項下：「狻猊出香亦翡色也，上爲蹲獸，下有仰蓮以承之，諸器唯此物最精絕。其餘則越州古秘色，汝州新窯器，大槩相類。」徐兢出使高麗是在宣和五年，是韓國高麗青瓷製作最成熟的時代，而其書於宣和六年撰進（西元一一二四年），亦即北宋結束之前一年。而竟沒提及頗具份量的北宋官窯，令人不免產生北宋官窯是否存在的疑問。又南宋周密的武林舊事，記載南宋高宗時進貢之貴重物品有商周銅器及汝窯器，若如顧文薦所言北宋官窯爲京師置窯燒造者，則其貴重程度應不亞於汝窯，爲何略而不言。而最先提出「北宋官窯」之說的顧文薦在其記述的同一段文字中，言及邵成章在高宗南渡後提舉後苑，造青器。事實上，根據最近沙孟海氏「南宋官窯脩內司窯址問題的商榷」一文的考證，邵成章雖曾爲徽宗內侍，後被除名，放逐南雄州，終其生未能還朝。因此「中興渡江」「提舉後苑」燒造南宋脩內司官窯之記載，全屬訛傳不符史實。顧氏爲南宋末人，撰文時距北宋已有一百多年，故所述及之「北宋官窯」的真實性仍待考。相較之下，徐兢、周密這二則資料均出自與朝廷關係較密切之人之手，時代也近，因此其可憑信度亦當較高。

以上有關北宋官窯之史料及院藏實物之情形都存有相當的商榷性，是今後陶瓷史研究的一項重要課題。至於南宋官窯，在宋末、元、明以至於清乾隆爲止，有關的記載亦不同於顧氏文中有明確脩內司官窯及郊壇下官窯之分的記述。如宋趙彥衛所著「雲麓漫鈔」（成書於一二〇六年）中記有「青瓷器，皆云出自李王，號秘色，又云出錢王，今處之龍溪出者，色粉青，越艾色……。近臨安亦自燒之，殊勝二處。」文中稱青瓷器出自李王，但不知是否指唐之李。又云出錢王，此乃吳越之錢氏，故應屬於越州窯（唐代越州之青瓷因茶經的記載而著名。）越州之青瓷與宋龍泉所產之青瓷，一爲氧化焰一爲還原焰，而在趙彥衛文中已能將其色辨爲艾與粉青，並稱近臨安亦自燒之，且勝於這二處，著實不易！臨安是指南宋京畿所在，文中雖未稱南宋官窯，但提到"自燒之"當必是臨安首府自燒之，趙文中提及青瓷系列都屬越州境內燒製，在其同時代只提及燒造地點之地名臨安，而無脩內司官窯及郊壇下官窯之分。

及至元朝，在「至正直記」中有「乙未冬（西元一三五五年）在杭州時，市哥哥洞窯者，一香鼎，質細雖新，其色瑩潤如舊造，識者猶疑之。會荊溪王德翁亦云：近日哥哥窯絕類古官窯，不可不細辨」。由這則元朝的記載，文中不但提出官窯的名稱，而且加上「古」字。而且也知道這個時期的哥窯燒造得絕類古官窯。當然此文中只稱「官窯」，並未如顧氏之三分官窯的稱法。由於這則資料的官、哥記載而形成後世「官哥不分是一家」之說。

到了明朝，「格古要論」一書中論及古窯器，官窯項下記「宋脩內司燒者土脈細潤，色青帶粉紅，濃淡不一，有蟹爪紋，紫口鐵足，色好者與汝窯相類，有黑土者謂之烏泥窯，偽者皆龍泉燒者，無紋路。」另外哥窯項下記有「舊哥窯，色青濃淡不一，亦有鐵足紫口，色好者類董窯，今亦少有成群隊者，元末新燒者，土脈燥，色亦不好。」從這兩段記載可看出將官窯稱修內司燒者，並指出以「紫口鐵足」爲其口緣及圈足之特徵，並沒有脩內司官窯及郊壇下官窯之分。文中並且指出龍泉窯所燒造的仿官釉作品，其釉無開片。對於哥窯，則記有舊哥窯與元末新燒者，其特色則以「鐵足紫口」稱之，正好與官窯之「紫口鐵足」相同的文字但排列秩序有前後之不同，不知是否另具含意在。以本院所藏的實物而言，如展品2號，10號，35號，45號，59號，68號等等，雖有薄胎薄釉者，亦有薄胎厚釉等之不同；開片有大有小，且或具冰裂紋者；然皆屬紫金土胎土，圈足平整自然，在燒造前，圈足底都沒特意加一層鐵水，露胎處呈自然的黑褐色，釉質皆瑩潤。口緣部份僅稍呈流釉現象，但並沒有特別明顯露出口緣的胎色呈明顯的紫口。或口緣之色澤因釉較器身薄而略呈紫，格古要論中將其稱紫口鐵足來強調南宋官窯的特色，而這個特徵的強調也指引了後世仿官窯作品的方向。如展品62號筆筒，其圈足底鏃成圓脊狀，並塗上一層鐵水使其燒成後呈褐黑而亮的色澤。在口緣處未上釉之前，先塗一道褐色彩，使其口緣色加深，然後上釉，釉燒成時口緣稍呈流釉，而其釉薄處便顯出特別的紫口鐵足的效果。這件依風格來看可能是清朝之作。而展品1號花盆則是在燒成後，沿口緣塗上一道淺褐色，可能是膠一類的物質，看起來亦呈紫口的效果。後世用不同方法製作的仿品，重點皆在紫口鐵足，可能是受格古要論這段文字的影響。

在此附帶一提，前述至正直記中所言「近日哥哥窯絕類古官窯，不可不細辨。」一句，其記述年代爲一三五五年，距元朝結束僅十三年。而格古要論成書於洪武二十一年，距至正直記只有三十三年，但論及元末新燒的哥窯則是「土脈燥，色亦不好」。兩者對哥窯的品評有很大的差距，當然這可能由於作者主觀的鑑賞標準的不同而造成的。但却可從這兩則資料中得知，在元朝時對於南宋官窯，哥窯相類似的觀念已形成。因此在明萬曆十九年高濂「遵生八牋」中有「官窯品格大率與哥窯相同」的話。時序推移，距宋朝愈遠對於官窯的看法也愈與哥窯相混淆。到了清朝谷應泰的「博物要覽」中記載的官窯爲：「官窯者燒於宋修內司中，爲官家造也。窯在杭州鳳凰山下，其土紫故足色若鐵，時云紫口鐵足，紫口乃「器口上仰」「釉水流下」，比周身淺，故口露紫痕，此何足貴，惟尚鐵足以他處土咸不及此也。」文中特別提到窯在杭州鳳凰山下，南宋皇城城南主峰爲鳳凰山，故稱窯在鳳凰山下，在此可明確地看出這則資料中所稱的官窯是指南宋，但却沒將其作修內司官窯、郊壇下官窯之分。但是到了清「稗史類編」所記述的則與負喧雜錄之內容相似；「郊壇下別立新窯亦曰官窯，比之舊窯大不侔矣」。另外在清乾隆三十九年朱琰所著的「陶説」卷二古窯考中，除了錄有汝窯外，並列有「宋官窯」及「宋脩內司官窯」，其內容爲：「宋官窯，宋政和間，京師自置窯燒造，曰官窯。」另有「宋修內司官窯，宋南渡，有邵成章，提舉號邵局，襲舊京造製，置窯於修內司，造青器，曰內窯，亦曰官窯。」亦在此文之後並將博物要覽及稗史類編之記載附錄於後，其所述的宋官窯及宋脩內司官窯皆可看出是據顧文薦之文而來，但却沒另立條目列舉郊壇下官窯。這是否意味著作者已有己見 ?!

綜觀上述所舉的歷代資料，不難發現，除了顧文薦的記載，在元、明二代，皆無北宋官窯、南宋脩內司、郊壇下官窯之名目，但到了清朝，有關陶瓷資料的彙編整理漸盛，凡記述宋官窯則多以顧氏之文爲本，因而演變成對宋官窯三分法的固定觀念。沙孟海氏基於近年杭州郊壇下窯址的挖掘與調查，重新對文獻資料做深入地考證，認爲「有關南宋官窯的記載比較可以信靠的，只有宋理宗，咸淳四年（公元一二六八年）知臨安軍府事潛説友所纂臨安志（世稱咸淳臨安志）。此是官書，傳世尚存九十六卷。自第一卷至十五卷首行在所錄，記述宮廷建置及設官分職最爲詳備⋯⋯。第十卷內諸司下臚列：入內內侍省" 皇城司 "" 御藥院 "" 內東門司 "" 天章閣 "" 後苑 "" 御前庫 "等三十三個官署。其中第十八個官署就是" 提舉修內司 "，下注" 在孝仁坊內青平山口 "。第十九個官署是" 御前內轄司”，下注“在東華門外東庫內”。次行低一格列敘下級七個單位，即“東庫”“西庫”“南庫”“北庫”“青器窰”“八作司”“教樂所”。青器窰下注“在雄武營山上圓壇左右”……。最值得注意的是咸淳臨安志並未記載青器窰有兩處。更未説一處在圓壇左右，另一處在修內司內。根據這些資料，我們便可下一結論：照今天的説法，修內司是機關，不是窰場，青器窰才是窰場。」

　　而前文已提到顧文薦記邵成章提舉後苑置窰燒造青器與史實不符，今再比對臨安志所記修內司官窰與郊壇下官窰的説法恐也有出入。

　　依上述情形觀之，到北宋爲止，窰產品的稱呼仍襲唐朝以燒造所在地之地名而名之。宋著名的汝窰在文獻中被稱「汝窰宮中禁燒」，因供宮中御用而特別燒造，同時代的徐兢在其書內亦強調，仍只稱新汝器。而南宋杭州的官窰則是承宮中之命才開窰燒造，不是在已經生產陶瓷有年的窰來搭便定燒作部份的宮中用品，基於這種特質，所以才稱「官窰」，而不以窰址所在的臨安稱呼。這種以其特殊用途作窰名的應該是自「官窰」始，因此宋代五大名窰中之官、哥，其時期應屬南宋。而五大名窰中又以汝窰及官窰最受珍重。武林舊事記汝窰在南宋陸游的「老學庵筆記」也提到「故都時定器不入禁中，唯用汝器。」這些都證明汝窰雖十分貴重，作爲宮中器用，但仍以產地名稱之。近年汝窰窰址在河南開封西南的寶豐縣清涼寺村發現，當地除了生產宮中御用之精緻青瓷外，亦有其他產品。因此「汝窰宮中禁燒」，是當時文人所知的一面而已，其雖俱「宮中禁燒」之尊，但亦以窰產地之地名稱之。到了南宋，方志上所記載的「青器窰」，屬提舉修內司管轄，設於雄武山圓壇左右，離皇城不遠，新闢一窰，有其專屬，這意味著燒造宮中所須瓷器之特殊性。因此雲麓漫沙所記之「臨安亦自燒之」，其「自燒之」的意義應是重點。以上在在皆可看出北宋汝窰與南宋官窰屬同具「官窰」之性質，但在燒造的基本環境有所不同。

　　主持南宋官窰田野調查工作的朱伯謙氏指出「瓷場的布局是，工房在山的平地上，龍窯建在烏龜山的西坡，規模比較大，窯房有做坯用的紫金土礦，取材方便，東北距皇城僅二公里，聯繫比較方便，但不受污水與烟火的影響。建窯的條件比萬松嶺等地優越。尤其重要的是，在窯址中發現大量的早晚二種產品，即南宋前期的薄胎薄釉青瓷與南宋後期的薄胎厚釉青瓷。薄胎薄釉青瓷，胎骨很薄，質地細膩，呈灰黑或深灰色。……釉色以粉青為主，也有青灰，青黃和蜜臘等色。由于通體薄釉，裝窯時坯件與匣體之間用支釘支燒。燒成後外底留有圓形的釘痕。……另外，在烏龜山西坡發現龍窯二座，龍窯的使用期限較長，南宋立國一百五十年，在這期間，先後用二座龍窯燒瓷是完全可以的……。」這個挖掘報告似乎可以確定南宋官窯窯址的情形。但是據上海硅酸鹽研究所稱：「曾經在地藏殿後邊發現一件六個支釘的圓形支墊窯具。」這是一個支節問題，地藏殿亦在鳳凰山麓。須待日後對鳳凰山一帶，特別是萬松嶺等地做詳細的調查，是否還有其他南宋燒造官窯窯址的存在，使南宋官窯只在郊壇下一地燒造之說更能釐清。

以上將有關宋官窯的一些資料加以探討。現就此次特展的實物略做檢討，本院藏品名為北宋官窯這一類中，在器型、製作方面都令人有相當的疑問。早在一九三〇年代陶瓷在系統性的研究風氣漸盛之際，英國戴維德氏便認為顧文薦的記載前段「汝州青瓷窯」與後文的「宣政間京師自置窯燒造名曰官窯」應屬一事。故北宋汝窯應即是普通名詞的北宋官窯，此外別無專有名詞的北宋官窯，這個看法早年即為部份人士所接受。在本展67，68號展品葵花式小盌，薄胎薄釉，釉略呈半失透釉。盌之口緣及器身的曲線非常俐落，在釉質方面氣泡較少，感覺上較近汝窯。雖名稱為北宋官窯，但其胎色與展品35號簋式爐比較則色澤較淡，呈深灰色，胎質亦稍堅。南宋官窯的胎土據研究報告稱：「胎土中氧化硅含量在65%左右，比越窯青瓷低，氧化鋁在20%以上，最高的達28%，氧化鐵含量亦在2%以上，最高的達4.22%，鋁與鐵的含量都比較高，很可能是用瓷石與紫金土兩種原料配製而成，目的是制成薄胎瓷器。」據該文，胎土的瓷石與紫金土之配合比例或在南宋的早、中、晚期有所不同，早期的瓷石可能比晚期的瓷石比例要高些，這與釉的厚薄相關連，紫金土之比例愈高則胎色愈呈黑。在本院所藏的宋官窯胎色自然者，有一個跡象即其色愈黑釉則愈厚，因此展品67、68號二件呈深灰色，薄胎薄釉似應屬南宋早期之作品。本展80、81、82、83號洗之類胎薄釉厚，開片多，常呈冰裂紋，釉內氣泡較多，呈大小不均，器型線條柔順流暢，稜角明顯，胎皆呈黑褐色，圈足露胎處沒有特意塗上鐵水加重色，（即一般所稱之護胎釉）。上述的這些宋官窯，歷來都與汝窯相同地非常受重視。然而，此類型的宋官窯青瓷在墓葬及窖藏中仍未發現，當然由於宋皇室之墓葬情況至今未明，不能置喙。但是以宋朝的名窯而言，定窯、鈞窯、龍泉窯、建窯等都有非常好的精品在墓葬中出土，唯獨汝、官未見有確定的例子出現，這也可證明汝、官所具的特殊性格。至今為止可發現一些類似官窯型青瓷在墓葬及窖藏中出土，部份可供年代的參考，有部份則可供當時龍泉仿官的資料參考。現列舉於下：如浙江磐安縣安文鎮寺口村M2墓所發現的青瓷盤，據報告稱：高4.2公分，直徑9.2公分，釉色粉青，口與圈足一周不施釉，露出黑紫色胎，即所謂紫口鐵足，圈足上有支釘痕。其年代推定上限為北宋天聖年間。天聖年間是一○二三年至一○三一年，在這個期間黑紫色胎的青瓷是否已經有了，如是則窯口應在何處？而且在北宋的青瓷系列裏，口緣不施釉者除定窯之外似乎很少見。

另外在浙江吳興縣湖州南二十公里下昂集鎮北石泉村宋墓中出土一件青瓷杯，據報告稱：口徑為8.4公分，高6.5公分，呈粉青色，開片細小如冰裂，口沿和圈足均無釉，為醬色，俗有紫口鐵足之稱，應屬龍泉仿官產品。該墓推定年代為南宋晚期。龍泉窯仿官窯的有大窯新亭、嶴底、杉樹連山和溪口瓦窯墻、骷髏灣、李家山等。據報告稱以溪口瓦窯墻仿製官窯最多且最像。在本展41號灰青缽與上述青瓷杯類似，但尺寸要大些，另外一件84號葵瓣口小洗其釉質頗似官釉，有冰裂紋開片，胎色灰白，具明顯的龍泉窯特色，此已在故宮博物院出版的宋瓷圖錄中改為龍泉窯，因此而知，龍泉窯在南宋時燒造仿官窯的產品有二類：一為釉與胎皆仿，一為只仿釉而胎色照龍泉原本之灰白。本展41號這件灰青缽在口緣薄釉呈紫色，此種口緣流釉較明顯的情形與本展之67號及80至83號洗口緣流釉不甚明顯、圈足修法自然平整的情形不相似，釉質方面呈較稠的感覺但口緣稜處流釉明顯，蓋龍泉仿的官窯青瓷仍可看出其刻意製作之處。特別是本展110號之盌，在圈足露胎處可以看見為了顯出鐵足因而在圈足底上了一層深褐色，由此可知在龍泉仿官之作品，已注意到鐵足特色的表現。

最值得注意的是吳興縣城南十五公里的皇紋山山坡所發現的宋墓，陪葬品中有二件青瓷蓮瓣盌，據報告稱：「胎青紫色，口沿、圈足如胎色，胎質堅細，類似南宋官窯中的烏泥窯，口沿作六瓣蓮瓣形……。另又一件粉青把杯，釉色粉青，片紋如冰裂，口沿、圈足赤紫色，如俗稱紫口鐵足樣，把柄的斷折角邊由于釉水下注而成枯白，……此三件應屬於宋代官窯。」這三件器物的造型都很精美，與其他陪葬器物一樣造型典雅，具有宋代風格。其單把杯與本院所藏的鈞窯圓底單把杯造型相似。而其把柄的斷折角釉水下注處呈枯白，由於胎土灰白，稜角處釉薄的地方會呈青白，這即俗稱出筋，是龍泉窯產品的特徵，因此這件單把杯雖呈紫口鐵足但應屬於龍泉仿官之作品。而此墓據報告所推定的年代為北宋末或南宋初（即一一二六年前後），二件陪葬的青瓷蓮瓣盌之「口沿與圈足如胎色」，換言之即口沿與圈足無釉。在這段時期正好是宋徽宗因定窯口芒而命燒汝窯青器的時期，如果墓葬時間可確定，則為何在不作興芒口的時期，會有如此造型典雅的芒口青瓷之制作呢？或是在當時，已將要呈進宮的產品與非進宮之產品，在製作上有區分？或是為陪葬而製作之產品？等等都不得而知。據朱伯謙氏「談南宋官窯」一文中稱：「龍泉仿官的厚釉青瓷始燒年代應在西元一二〇〇年前後」。以該墓葬的年代，器物的窯口產地仍須進一步探討，以便尋求合理的解釋。

以上這些例子都是在浙江省境內所發現的。除了浙江省之外，在安徽省之安慶市發現了一個土窖穴，內有八件瓷器置於大陶罐中，其中有五件是青瓷，報告中指其皆「足底露胎，呈鐵黑色，口沿釉薄，呈絳紫色。」另有一件爲米黃釉盤，圈足內以六支釘燒，據稱是「景德鎮元朝仿南宋官窯」。這一類型與本展中118號至121號頗相似，底足薄釉支釘燒，但口緣爲葵花口，另有二件口緣明顯的流釉看似鑲銅口。此窖穴所出土的米黃把杯與本展75號相似，尺寸略大一些，釉質顯得較稠，有凝重的感覺。與其同出土之組合器物來看，有元朝的青花葵口盤、青花匜及上述之青瓷盤，器壁皆較平且外敞，此種器型在元朝常見，而釉質看來正介於官與哥之間。在元朝這個時期可能有一部份的仿官與哥窯的釉質相當接近。也可能因此而導至後世之所以言官、哥不分家的理由。

在明初洪武四年汪興祖墓葬中出土葵口青瓷盤，與元青花同組合出土，據南京市博物館清理報告中稱爲哥窯，有大、中、小三種尺寸共十一件。中者與本展79號相似，小者則與本展119號相近，開片情況亦相近，釉色略顯青。雖是明初墓葬出土但應爲元代之作品。另外在上海市青浦縣發現的元代任氏墓群中出土一件青瓷膽瓶及魚耳爐，造型與本展之45號及36號相類似。本展覽之雙耳爐釉質方面稠且凝重、口緣流釉呈薄釉露紫口，這一類可確定爲南宋末至元時代之釉質。此件可提供做元朝的官釉系統之參考資料。而膽瓶據汪慶正氏稱應爲宋朝之物。本展45號之膽瓶釉薄滋潤，制作謹嚴，其釉質的感覺與英國戴維德氏收藏中之撇口官窯瓶類似，但戴氏藏的一件造型要豐碩些。

綜觀以上所舉上海青浦市任氏墓群中出土之膽瓶及浙江吳興縣皇紋山之宋墓出土的二件蓮花口盌及一件粉青把杯等器，質地與造型都很精緻，但是否爲南宋官窯尚難確認。至今在墓葬中仍未見有南宋官窯精品的陪葬，（南宋皇室陵墓的情況，暫不論。）準此略可看出南宋官窯之特殊性，或由是而造成後世瓷器收藏者的愛重，亦促使了元、明、清皆有精緻的仿官之作，本院所藏的列爲宋官窯器中很明顯地由釉質，胎土皆可看出有一批製作謹然，圈足修得平整，或成圓脊狀，並有護胎釉，具清朝之風格，特別是有乾隆御題刻字的這一類都具有清代風格，特別是成對的如46、47及48、49號，雖然底的處理或釉色有不同之處，但仍爲同一釉質胎土，應是清朝之作。至於三登方壺成對之二件，以釉質而言稍呈稠狀，不似南宋官窯的釉質，而最有疑問的是其底足成圓脊狀。一件底部刻有乾隆御題，另一件則無。本展1號圈足修成階梯狀，圈足底非常平整，釉與胎之間的界線非常整齊，這種圈足的修法自康熙開始，其釉均勻且薄，有細開片，失透釉全面呈不自然無光狀，口緣上有燒成後才塗上的淺褐色（可能爲膠之類），在視覺上呈紫口的效果。此種釉薄均勻而呈失透的青瓷其釉面皆有經特別磨去光澤的處理在本展中有31號鬲式爐，76號八方盤，43號水仙盆，26號盤口穿帶瓶等。上述的這幾件除水仙盆外，其底足露胎處皆加重了一層鐵水。使其呈黑褐色之鐵足。至於水仙盆造型尺寸皆與本院所藏汝窯水仙盆相近，盆底支釘痕之排列亦相同。而本展之水仙盆支釘痕乍看呈褐黑色，但用放大鏡看，其支釘痕之黑褐色是燒成後才著的，原本的胎色應是灰白色。另外上述26號盤口穿帶弦紋瓶與25號在造型尺寸方面很相近，25號這件釉厚瑩亮，有大開片，片紋經染色，其圈足底修成圓脊狀，且加重一層鐵水著色，又黑又亮，此類圈足在本展中不少。25號這件釉質及圈足之修法，屬清雍正、乾隆時代仿汝、仿官的樣式。而25號與26號在釉質與重量方面兩者截然不同，但經X光透視，發現兩者製造上接胎的情況完全一樣，腹部一接，頸部中間一接，以三片形成的。由這二件便可以體會到清雍正、乾隆朝仿官，曾用盡心思在釉與胎上面下了很大的功夫。在盤口弦紋穿帶壺這類器以22號之釉與製作顯得較自然，但是在仔細觀察其圈足露胎處可明顯地看出在圈足底塗上一層褐黑色，以成鐵足之效果，而且圈足修得不整，最大的疑問點在於胎重且在瓶內底平坦與器身之間有凹狀存在，這種現象在雍正乾隆時的御器廠所燒造的彩瓷品中常見到。因此這一類盤口瓶所存的疑點相當大。

至於所展示的貫耳穿帶壺這一類18號之底接法非常特殊，八方形之身延至足底，再以另片內貼器身底成爲圈足底，這種作法如果說是因八方造形須以此法接底，但12號這件不是八方形橢圓壺而其底成圓形，亦以另片由足內接成器底。這二件的器身底皆成內凹狀，這二件釉質稍稠很相近，底足露胎，呈褐黑色稍淺，口緣流釉較明顯但沒有露胎，成紫口，這種作法在同型的器物如本展9號10號雖亦爲橢圓型，但其底與器身相連，呈平整狀，這二件釉質，胎色皆爲標準南宋官窯，由此可見12號與18號之作法非常特殊。同樣器底用另片銜接的還有一件53號八方稜形瓶，這三件釉質皆同，推測可能是在南宋官窯結束後所仿造的，因其只刻意於外觀的造形，而貼底屬於非常態生產之個別製作。其釉質屬較稠，近似上海青浦元朝任氏墓出土的簋式小爐，而且雜質含得更多些。由於其圈足底的處理自然，沒有特意上一層護胎釉，釉面光澤沒有經處理除去呈自然狀態，因此推測不會晚於清朝。至於具有清朝特色的如13號的杏紋方壺，此造型始自清朝。器體頗厚重，足底修得非常平整，釉亮潔光瑩。11號貫耳穿帶方壺釉質及胎皆與25號盤口穿帶壺相同，在造型上雖勻整但線條太鋒利，不似宋朝之作。

本展的葵瓣口洗一類中，都以六支釘燒，但口緣有八瓣，九瓣及十瓣所成的花口，其釉質的感覺亦各有不同，在時代上可能亦不同。而葵花口盤的這一類，有些爲支釘燒，有些爲圈足，支釘燒的這類時代可能早些，但這二類由其釉質及器形來看皆爲南宋以後所燒造的。如上述明洪武汪興祖墓中所出土的盤就與本展79號，119號類似。另本展中38號是件非常有趣的青瓷，胎厚釉厚，器身非常重，釉大開片，圈足露胎處呈黑褐色，以鐵水加重色澤，在露胎的圈足底外，圈足內底有五個凸出圓錐形且光滑的支釘，無釉亦呈黑褐色，開片有大小二種，開片有染色，本展中開片特意染色者大部份非南宋之作品，器底有陽文無釉二字款，上字似爲中，下字爲丞。應爲「中丞」二字，推測可能與康熙時郎廷極任江西巡撫，監督景德鎮御窯時，其友許謹齋有詩「癸巳年下郎窯戲紫衡中丞」有關，此件爐的造型與本院所藏的康熙款之冰梅銅胎琺瑯相似，這種造形在康熙之青花爐亦常見到。本展這件青瓷爐，依其情況觀應是工匠只依傳聞中所述宋官窯爲：厚釉、支釘燒、紫口鐵足之文字資料來仿宋官窯，並未能親睹宋官窯而仿的情況下所製造出來的，故令人覺得可愛有趣。由本院所藏列爲宋官窯的這批青瓷而言。我們可以由幾件比較特殊的，做爲根據，以其釉質、胎土及造形或製造方面，判斷其爲元、明、清之仿造，借此而作進一步的比對，以瞭解全部的藏品之情形，其中有一些具有相當明顯的特徵，比較容易辨識，亦有一些在定位上相當困難，尤其是南宋末及元朝的情形仍未確定，官窯在整個南宋歷時一百多年間，因時代的推移，窯的盛衰給予製作的影響，未能十分把握。由本院所藏的名爲宋官窯藏品中只能推測，南宋末至元這一段時間可能在品質上已日漸趨弱，但其實際的情況及範圍應包括到什麼樣的程度，只得等待杭州窯址的調查報告以明實況。由此次的宋代官窯特展可以體會到，南宋官窯盛期美好的產品，比想像中要少。也藉此次的官窯特展得知自清朝乾隆以後，由於對陶瓷鑑賞風氣的盛行普及一般士大夫、中產階級，但由於元、明時代有關記載與實物傳承不多,仿品却層出不斷的情況下,因而引起了種種臆説，致使南宋官窯的系列中，滲進了後期的仿品。這當然是因時空的局限及認知的程度問題，但本院能有這一系列的青瓷同藏於一處，是提供研究最佳的資料，希望日後能承方家指引，對近千年以前的宋代官窯之實際情況能更進一步地去研究、瞭解。

中華民國七十七年九月成稿

# AN OVERVIEW OF THE EXHIBITION
# OF SUNG DYNASTY KUAN WARE

## by Ts'ai Ho-pi

The 143 pieces displayed in this exhibition are arranged according the National Palace Museum's traditional nomenclature, which divides Kuan ware into three distinct types: 1) Northern Sung Kuan ware, 2) Southern Sung *Hsiu-nei-ssu* Kuan ware and 3) Southern Sung *Chiao-t'an-hsia* Kuan ware.

The National Palace Museum Collection of Sung dynasty Kuan ware is exceptional in both its quantity and its quality. The especially fine pieces from this vast collection have been chosen for this exhibit; let us start by briefly surveying a few of the more outstanding of these. Note, for example, piece #67, a floral-shaped bowl, with its thin and delicate paste and glaze and the gentle beauty of the lines in the mallow-petal mouth-rim. Then there are brush washers, such as piece #58, which were used to adjust the quantity and density of ink in a painter's or calligrapher's brush as he worked; this hibiscus-shaped piece is exceptionally exquisite and unusual in overall effect, with the pronounced angles of the rim, the clearly differentiated leveling, the thin layer of glaze on the natural dark-brown paste and the slight purple of the "glaze-flow" (exposure of the paste due to down-flowing of the glaze) at the vertices of the angles. Piece #8, a vase with tubular handles and hooped decor made in the shape of the ancient bronze vessel known as a *hu,* is 38.2 cm. tall, making it the largest known vessel of its type. The thick walls, relatively large proportioned handles and full round belly combine to produce an impression of harmonious largesse. The round basins displayed as pieces #80, #81, #82, #83, #88 and #90, gentle and dignified in effect, all have traces on the bottom of the supports or washers used to prop them up during firing; the glaze on these pieces is thicker and more translucent than that on pieces #58, #67 and #68. Pieces #9 and #10 are *hu* shaped vases with hooped decor, a stable and balanced appearance, and a natural uncolored crackle effect to the glaze, which culminates in an ice-crackle effect where the glaze is thick and a slight purple appearance at the rim, where the glaze is thin due to glaze-flow. The rim of piece #2, a vase in the form of a bronze *tsun,* appears somewhat incongruous with respect to the overall form; it could be that the metal rim was added after the original everted lip was slightly damaged. The elegant form of this vessel is covered with a thick and glossy glaze, which gives an especially lovely green appearance at its thickest spots. The glaze on piece #35, an incense burner in the shape of a bronze *kuei,* is comparable in beauty, perhaps even more beautiful, creating an unparalleled feeling of mystery and depth. Some glaze appears to have dripped downwards underneath the handles during the firing process, resulting in an accumulation of glaze that had to be sanded away, revealing the dark purple paste underneath. The wholeness and integrity effected between the round foot and the oval mouth on this piece indicate great maturity of technique. Piece #44, a large rectangular pot with thick walls and a thick glaze with layered ice-crackles, is as elegant and refined as pieces #2 and #35, despite its size. Dishes such as pieces #98, #99, #100, #101 and #102 are all first class works, with their graceful floral mouth-rims and angled waists. Bowls such as pieces #103, 106 and #107, with their rounded bellies and floral mouth-rims, provide a harmonious match to the dishes and other vessels. The most exquisite of all the lobed vessels with foliated rims displayed in this exhibit are probably the dishes displayed as piece #92, modeled in the shape of a caltrop, #93, in the shape of a lotus blossom, #94, in the shape of a peony, and #95, in the shape of a chrysanthemum. All of the above achieve a high-water mark of elegance and grace.

Most of the Sung and Yüan porcelain in the National Palace Museum was gathered into the imperial collection during three early reigns of the Ch'ing dynasty, namely the K'ang-hsi (1662-1722), Yung-cheng (1722-1735) and Ch'ien-lung (1735-1795) periods. In the early K'ang-hsi period (1662-1682), Ts'ao Hsi, great-grandfather of Ts'ao Hsüeh-chin, author of *The Dream of the Red Chamber (Hung-lou Meng* 紅樓夢 ), kept a list of the paintings, calligraphy, porcelain ware and curios presented as tributes to the court. From this list it is clear that the Manchu emperors of the Ch'ing dynasty, after taking over the Forbidden City from the Ming rulers and consolidating their empire, gradually began to take an interest in the masterpieces of Chinese art left by the former tenants, and even in improving and adding to the imperial collection thereof. This was expecially true of the Ch'ien-lung Emperor, who, since his empire was rich and strong and his own level of artistic cultivation high, collected more renowned artworks as tribute gifts than any other emperor. Under these conditions, not only the genuine Kuan ware made in the Sung dynasty, but also the imitations of Kuan ware made by the Lung-ch'üan kiln in Sung dynasty and other kilns throughout the Yüan and Ming were presented to the court, due to the limited discrimitative abilities of those offering tribute. In this exhibit, beautiful and exquisitely made examples of both the genuine Sung Kuan ware and these imitations have been selected for display, so as to provide a richer comparative perspective from which to understand the entire Kuan and Kuan glaze line of wares. This essay will also provide an explanation of the implications and meanings of the term "Kuan ware." At the same time, an attempt will be made to examine and discuss the relevant references in the historical records, so as to allow us to contemplate Kuan ware with a higher degree of clarity.

The term "Kuan ware" has both a broad and a narrow meaning, corresponding to its use as a common descriptive word and as a special proper noun. The broad common meaning refers to any pieces made by official governmental order for use in the imperial court, the word *kuan* meaning literally "official; pertaining to governmental office." The "Ch'ü-chi" chapter of the *Li Chi* states, "The Son of Heaven has six types of craftsmen: clay-workers, stone-workers, wood-workers, animal trainers and gardeners." ("Clay-work" means ceramics and pottery.) All the above types of handicrafts were considered "official (*kuan*) crafts." The *T'ang liu-tien* states, "An official post is to be created for a director of pottery, to be ranked in the lowest third of stratum eight." The *Chiu T'ang-shu* records, "The Pottery Office consists of one Director, two Aides, five Storehouse Overseers, ten Subofficial Functionaries, four Work Supervisors and 18 Managers. They are in charge of producing crafted stone and clay works . . . ." The official craftsmen referred to in these sources devoted themselves exclusively to the production of *objects d'art* for use in the imperial court. Pieces not made by specific official order could also sometimes be accepted as tribute gifts, and hence as types of "kuan ware," but only if they were the cream of the crop of a particular area's local specialty. An example of this practice is recorded in the *T'ang Liu-tien*, which states: "The Hopei Circuit presented Hsing-chou pottery as tribute." The pottery repeatedly offered by the Ch'ien family of Wu-yüeh in the early Sung dynasty is another example. Another is recorded in the third *chüan* of Wang Ts'un's Sung dynasty work *Yüan-feng chiu-yü chih*, which states, "Fifty pieces of pottery were donated by the magistrate of Hua-Yüan prefecture in Yao-chou." Once a local specialty was accepted into the imperial court as a tribute gift, it too came to be regarded as a type of "kuan ware." All of the above examples can be considered "kuan ware" according to the broad, common-usage definition, as can all works made by imperial craftsmen or not for general circulation; the latter category included both wares submitted to the court regularly, for example annually, and those given only on special occasions, as in the case of those kilns that "gave tribute when ordered, and didn't when not ordered." In the Ming and Ch'ing dynasties an imperial pottery kiln was established in Ching-te-chen, managed by specialists, and devoted solely to producing pottery for imperial use. After 1681, when an official was assigned by the Palace Treasury to ensure regular provision of funds to the imperial kiln, the regularly-submitted type of kuan ware became increasingly prominent. In the late Ch'ien-lung period (1736-1795) the supervision of its production was given over to the office of the Fu-liang County Administrator, which retained jurisdiction until the end of the Ch'ing dynasty. The meaning of "kuan ware" gradually narrowed. In this period, T'ao Ya wrote, "The choicest pieces of kuan ware are called Yü ware ("imperial ware"). Yü ware is what is used by the emperor himself, while the kuan ware is for the use of consorts and court ladies, and those ranked below them." The early Republican Period (1911-present) work *Yin-liu chai shuo-ts'u* states, "Yü ware was one of the types of kuan ware in the Ch'ing dynasty, made specially for use by the emperor and which no one else dared to touch. Kuan ware perse, on the other hand, can be used by anyone holding government office." From these historical sources we can get an overall impression of the wide range of meanings subsumed by the broad definition of kuan ware.

Taken according to its narrow definition as a proper noun, however, Kuan ware refers to the products of one specific kiln of the Sung dynasty (960-1280). The five most renowned ceramic wares of the Sung came from the Ting, Ju, Ko, Chün and Kuan kilns. The earliest references to the Kuan kiln can be found in the *Shuo-fu's* record of the late Southern Sung writer Ku Wen-chien's work *Fu-hsüan tsa-lu,* and in the *Ch'o-keng lu's* record of Yeh Chih's work *T'an-chai pi-heng.* These two references are worded almost identically, and since Yeh Chih's identity and dates are unknown it is impossible to say which came first. Here we will quote the reference as it appears in Ku Wen-chien's work: "The present administration judged the white porcelain of Ting-chou unfit for use, and thus ordered (the kilns in) Ju-chou to produce celadon ware. Thereafter the kilns in T'ang-chou in Hopei, Teng-chou and Yao-chou all followed this order. Ju ware is the finest of them all, whereas the materials from the Lung-ch'üan district kiln of Ch'u-chou in Kiangnan are somewhat coarse and thick. In the Hsüan-cheng period (1111-1125), a kiln was established in the capital itself to fire porcelain, called Kuan ware. After the movement of the capital across the river (i.e. the beginning of the Southern Sung in 1127), a certain Shao Ch'eng-chang was put in charge of production in the Rear Garden, which came to be called Shao's Bureau, and which adopted the system that had been used in the old capital. A kiln was established in Hsiu-nei-ssu to make celadon ware, called Inner ware (*nei-yao*) and made by use of refined-clay moulds, creating an extremely exquisite effect. The color is clear and transparent, and greatly treasured by the present generation. Later a new kiln was set up in Chiao-t'an-hsia, but its products were a far cry from those of the old kiln. Other wares such as Wu-ni ware, Yü-yao ware and Hsü ware do not compare with Kuan ware. As for the old Yüeh kilns, they no longer exist."

Here we have a reference to Kuan ware by a writer of the Sung era, categorizing it into three major types: Northern Sung Kuan ware, Southern Sung Hsiu-nei-ssu Kuan ware and Southern Sung Chiao-t'an-hsia Kuan ware. But there is not the slightest reference in any other source to any such trifold classification for the next six hundred years, that is, from the Southern Sung to the Ch'ien-lung period (1736-1795) of the Ch'ing dynasty. It was not until the late Ch'ing that this work of Ku Wen-chien's began to receive any attention, and it soon came to be quoted in Ch'ing sources in almost precisely the same words. This categorization of Kuan ware into three types-Northern Sung, Southern Sung Hsiu-nei-ssu and Southern Sung Chiao-t'an-hsia—was adopted therefrom and is still used to the present day. However, due to increasing attention to archaeological research and the attendant broadening of the scope of excavation in recent times, a great many famous T'ang and Sung kiln sites have been discovered, including the Ju ware kiln-site at Ch'ing-liang-ssu in Pao-feng county, Honan; and the Southern Sung Kuan ware kiln-site in the Chiao-t'an-hsia region of Hangchow, the excavations of which have already begun. These sites occupy an extremely important place in the history of Chinese ceramics, and their excavations promise to give us a more accurate knowledge of that history. Most of the Sung Kuan ware in the National Palace Museum collection, on the other hand, was received into the imperial collection in the early Ch'ing dynasty, some 600-700 years after the end of the Sung. The growing obscurity of and unfamiliarity with Kuan ware brought by this span of time, together with the greatly divergent standards used to accept tribute gifts in different periods and the prevalence of imitation porcelain in the Ch'ing period combined to produce much confusion and a great divergence of views about Kuan ware among modern scholars.

In the present essay we will attempt to introduce and analyze some of the historical references to Kuan ware, comparing this information with the pieces known to us from the National Palace Museum collection, so as to gain an understanding of how Sung Kuan ware was viewed over the ages. Let us start with what Ku Wen-chien classified as Northern Sung Kuan ware. Ku stated that "...in the Hsüan-cheng period, a kiln was established in the capital itself to fire porcelain, called Kuan ware." In accordance with this statement, all sources discussing porcelain production after the Ch'ien-lung period assume that both Ju ware and Northern Sung Kuan ware were used in the Northern Sung court. According to this text, the kiln should have been located in the capital, in other words in the Kaifeng region, and the materials used for the paste and glaze should have been those characteristic of Honan. However, in examining the pieces in the National Palace Museum collection which are registered in the original ledger as "Northern Sung Kuan ware," we find that the glaze is consistently semi-transparent with very few bubbles. The thickness of the glaze differs from piece to piece, and the glaze colors include sky-blue, green-blue, bluish-grey and moon white. The designs and techniques used on the rims and ring-feet also show great variation. The paste used for the bodies of these pieces is of a number of colors not commonly found in the Honan region, including off-white, dark grey and dark brown. Careful examination reveals that the only characteristics shared by all the pieces registered under this name are the semi-transparent glaze and the paucity of bubbles. Because the Kaifeng area is prone to frequent flooding, and since the loess soil in this region is layered up very thick, no large-scale archaeological excavation work has yet been conducted there. Whether or not there are remains of a Northern Sung Kuan ware kiln-site there, and whether the remains of its products would correspond to the pieces in the National Palace Museum collection, is as yet unknown.

The *Hsüan-ho feng-shih Kao-li t'u-ching* is another source from the Sung period which features a number of records concerning porcelain of the time, including Ting ware, Yüeh-chou ware and Ju-chou new ware, but makes no reference to Kuan ware. Under the heading of "Vessels," a number of shapes and designs are described, including an entry for "Ceramic Incense Burner" which reads in part, "The fragrance is emitted from a lion, which is also emerald in color, with a crouching animal on top and a lotus blossom on the bottom supporting it. Of all the vessels, this is the most remarkable and exquisite. Of the others, the old Yüeh-chou archaic celadon and the new Ju-chou ware are generally similar." Hsü Ching, the author of this work, was sent on his expedition to Korea in 1123, and the book came out the following year, one year before the end of the Northern Sung period. Under these circumstances, the fact that the work does not mention Northern Sung Kuan ware, supposedly produced in considerable quantity at this time, arouses serious doubts concerning the existence of this ware. Furthermore, the Southern Sung work *Wu-lin chiu-shih* by Chou Mi records that under the Kao-tsung Emperor (r. 1127-1162) the most valued of the tribute gifts in the court were Shang and Chou dynasty bronze vessels and Ju ware porcelain; if, as Ku stated, Northern Sung Kuan ware was made by a kiln in the imperial capital itself, it should not have been considered less valuable than Ju ware; why then is it not mentioned here?

Ku Wen-chien, the first writer known to have made reference to Northern Sung Kuan ware, in the same paragraph mentions that Shao Ch'eng-chang was put in charge of celadon production in the Rear Garden after the capital was moved south. However, a very different picture is painted by modern scholarship, for example in Sha Meng-hai's "On the Question of the Site of the Southern Sung Hsiu-nei-ssu Kuan Ware Kiln"(*Nan-Sung Kuan-yao Hsiu-nei-ssu yao wen-t'i ti Shang-ch'üeh* 南宋官窯脩內司窯址問題的商榷). According to Sha's research, although the eunuch Shao Ch'eng-chang did indeed serve the Hui-tsung Emperor (r. 1101-1125), he was eventually dismissed from his post and exiled to Nan-hsiung-chou, never again to return to the court. Thus it is clear the Ku's testimony that this man was put in charge of firing porcelain in the Rear Garden after the movement of the capital south is clearly contradicted by the known historical facts. Ku lived in the late Southern Sung and his book was written over a hundred years after the end of the Northern Sung period; thus the reliability of his testimony concerning the existence of Northern Sung Kuan ware is also open to serious doubt. The works of Hsü Ching and Chou Mi cited above come from the hands of men with comparatively intimate relations with the court and who lived closer in time to the events described. Thus the latter sources are to be considered more reliable.

The relation between the historical material on Northern Sung Kuan ware and the extant objects in the National Palace collection is still fairly controversial, and constitutes an important topic for historical research. In addition, the case of Southern Sung Kuan ware also presents problems, and the related references in other sources from the late Sung through the Ch'ien-lung period of the Ch'ing dynasty also differ from Ku Wen-chien's clear and definite description dividing it into two types, the Hsiu-nei-ssu and the Chiao-t'an-hsia. For example, the Sung work *Yun-lu man-ch'ao* by Chao Yen-wei (published in 1206) states, "All celadon ware is said by some to have originated with King Li; it was called "the forbidden color" (*mi-se*). Others say it originated with King Ch'ien. Nowadays that which comes from Lung-hsi is powder-blue in color, while that from Yüeh-chou is olive-green.... Recently they in the vicinity of Lin-an have been making it themselves, surpassing the products of the two former places." It is unclear whether this "King Li" refers to the imperial family of the T'ang dynasty, who bore the surname Li. "King Ch'ien" seems to refer to the Ch'ien family of Wu-yüeh, which would make this product a type of Yüeh-chou ware (the celadon ware of Yüeh-chou in T'ang times became famous due to its mention in the "Classic of Tea." (*Ch'a-ching* 茶經 ). Yüeh-chou celadon and Sung Lung-ch'üan celadon ware differ in that the former used oxidized coloring and the latter reductionized coloring, and yet Chao Yen-wei's text says that their colors could be distinguished as olive green and powder blue; moreover the text states that it eventually began to be made in the vicinity of Lin-an, surpassing the products of the two former places. This is no mean feat. Lin-an refers to the region of the Southern Sung capital, and although the text does not use the term "Southern Sung Kuan ware," it does say "making it themselves," which seems to indicate that this ware was being made inside the capital by imperial kilns. This text says only that celadon ware was produced within the Yüeh-chou region, mentioning only a single kiln location, Lin-an, and making no reference to any division of Hsiu-nei-ssu and Chiao-t'an-hsia Kuan ware.

The Yüan dynasty (1277-1368) work *Chih-cheng chih-chi* records, "In the winter of the year [1355] in Hangchow, one Ko-ko-tung ware [i.e. Ko ware] incense cauldron was bought; although the fine material is new, its color is as clear and transparent as the old ware, such that one might not be able to tell the difference. Wang Te-weng of Ching-hsi has also said as much. The modern Ko-ko ware far exceeds the Kuan ware of olden times, and one must be aware of this difference." This source is noteworthy not only for directly using the term Kuan ware, but also in modifying it with "of olden times." Moreover it is asserted that the contemporary Ko ware far exceeded former Kuan ware in quality. Of course, this is still a far cry from the detailed classification into three types found in Ku Wen-chien's text. It is perhaps this reference to Ko and Kuan ware, compared as if belonging to a single category, that led to the later convention of regarding Ko ware and Kuan ware as two variant strains of a single type of porcelain ware.

The above is an examination of some historical materials related to Sung Kuan ware. Now, however, let us turn our attention to the pieces on display in this special exhibition. The shapes and manufacturing techniques evident in many of the pieces in the National Palace Museum collection catalogued as Northern Sung Kuan ware give us some reason to doubt the accuracy of their classification. Thus it seems fair to say that so-called Northern Sung Kuan ware is in reality none other than the Ju ware of the Northern Sung, and that no ware specifically known as Kuan ware, as a proper noun, was made in this period. This point of view has been accepted by some scholars for many years. As early as the 1930s, when systematic research into Chinese ceramics was slowly gaining prevalence, the English collector Percival David suggested that Ku Wen-chien's records of "the Ju-chou celadon kiln" and "the Kuan ware kiln established by the capital" might refer to one and the same thing. Pieces #67 and #68 in this exhibit, small thin-glazed eggshell mallow flower-shaped bowls with nearly-transparent glaze, are decorated with extremely deft curved lines both around the rims and on the body. Combined with the relatively few bubbles in the glaze, this gives an impression somewhat closer to that of Ju ware than Northern Sung Kuan ware, although they are classified as the latter. However, the clay of these pieces, as compared with the incense burner displayed as piece #35, is relatively dull and dilute in color, giving a dark grey appearance, and is somewhat harder and more rigid in consistency. According to laboratory research, the clay used for Southern Sung Kuan ware usually contains about 65% silica, which is less than that contained in Yüeh ware; its average aluminium oxide content is over 20%, with a maximum of 28%, while the average iron oxide content is also over 2% but with a maximum of 4.2%. This simultaneous presence of relatively high levels of both aluminium oxide and iron oxide is perhaps a result of the combined use of two raw materials, namely ordinary Kaolin clay and *tzu-chin-t'u*, with the intention of producing a paste capable of forming an eggshell-thin body for the pieces. The proportion of Kaolin clay to *tzu-chin-t'u* in the early and middle Southern Sung may have differed from that in the late Southern Sung; the Kaolin content in the early periods was perhaps higher, which could have affected the thickness of the glaze used. The higher the *tzu-chin-t'u* content, the blacker the clay will generally appear. This fact is evident in the pieces in the National Palace Museum collection, which are generally given a thicker glaze the darker their clay is; thus dark-grey, thin-glazed, eggshell pieces like #67 and #68 are probably products of the early Southern Sung. Thin-bodied, thick-glazed washers such as #80, #81, #82 and #83 show much use of crackling and ice crack effects and have relatively numerous bubbles of various sizes in the glaze. The lines of these vessels have a gentle and graceful fluency to them, with definite angles to the shape. The paste is brown and black, and no iron paint (so-called "paste-protective glaze") has been applied to the exposed paste on the ring-feet. Like Ju ware, Kuan ware pieces such as these have always been highly esteemed and treasured. Although no Kuan ware pieces of this type have been discovered in tombs or storage vaults thus far, we cannot draw any definitive conclusions from this, since the contents of Sung imperial tombs are not yet known. However, the special status and problem of Ju and Kuan ware is obvious from the fact that many excellent specimens of every other type of porcelain ware renowned in the Sung, i.e. Ting, Chün. Lung-ch'üan and Chien wares, have already been found in tomb excavations. However, several pieces resembling Kuan ware have been found in these excavations, many of which provide us with important clues for dating of styles and for an understanding of the Lung-ch'üan imitations of Kuan ware. For example, a celadon bowl discovered in tomb M2 in Ssu-k'ou ts'un, An-wen chen, in P'an-an County of Chekiang, was described in the excavation report as follows: ". . . 4.2 cm. tall, 9.2 cm. in diameter, with light blue glaze and exposed dark purple paste at the unglazed mouth-rim and ring-foot, creating the so-called purple-mouth iron-foot effect. Traces of supports used in firing are apparent on the ring-foot. The date of this vessel is uncertain, but it could not have come from earlier than the Sung dynasty T'ien-sheng period (1023-1031)." It is not known whether celadon ware made from dark purple paste was already prevalent at this time, and if so where the kilns producing such pieces were located. Moreover, it should be noted that in general Northern Sung celadon ware pieces very rarely have unglazed mouth-rims.

A celadon cup found in a Sung tomb located in Pei-shih ch'üan-ts'un, Hsia-an chi-chen, 20 kilometers south of Hu-chou in Wu-hsing hsien, Chekiang, was described in the excavation report as follows: ". . .8.4 cm. in diameter, 6.5 cm. tall, light blue in color, with tiny and delicate crackles resembling ice-crack technique, and no glaze on either the mouth-rim or the ring-foot, thus giving the dark-brownish effect commonly known as purple-mouth iron-foot. This seems to be a Lung-ch'üan imitation of Kuan ware." This tomb-site dates from the late southern Sung period. Kilns producing Lung-ch'üan imitations of Kuan ware were located in a number of places, such as Ta-yao-hsin-t'ing, Au-ti, Shan-shu lien-shan, Hsi-k'ou wa-yao ch'iang, Ku-lou-wan amd Li-chia-shan. Of these imitations, the kiln at Hsi-k'ou way-yao ch'iang reportedly produced in the greatest numbers and with the greatest quality." An example of such an imitation can be seen in piece #41 in this exhibit, a bluish grey glazed alms bowl, similar to the above-mentioned celadon cup but slightly larger. Another example is piece #84, a small mallow-petal shaped brush washer, the glaze on which is quite similar to Kuan glaze, with its ice crackle effect, but the off-white paste of which marks it as an obvious Lung-ch'üan product; in fact this piece has already been identified as Lung-ch'üan ware in the *Illustrated Catalogue of Sung Dynasty Porcelain in the National Palace Museum; Lung-ch'üan Ware, Ko Ware and Other Wares,* published by the National Palace Museum (1974). From this it is clear that the Lung-ch'üan kiln produced two different types of imitation Kuan ware in the southern Sung: one imitating both the glaze and paste of Kuan ware, and another imitating the Kuan glaze but using the original Lung-ch'üan off-white color for the paste. The thin layer of glaze on the mouth-rim of piece #41 creates a purplish color; this relatively obvious and deliberate glaze-flow effect differs from what we see on brush washers such as pieces #67, #68 and #80-83, where the glaze-flow on the mouth-rim is not so obvious and the ring-foot has a natural evenness to it. The glaze on these pieces has a more dense feel to it, except on the angles of the rim, where the glaze-flow is more obvious. Here we can see the care taken by the Lung-ch'üan craftsmen in their imitations of Kuan ware. This is especially true of such items as piece #110, where a dark brown coloring was deliberately added to the exposed paste of the ring-foot to bring out the "iron-foot" effect. Thus it is clear that the Lung-ch'üan craftsmen had noticed the characteristic dark color of the "iron-foot" on Kuan ware, and had paid special attention to imitating it.

Two lotus-petal celadon bowls found among the burial pieces in the Sung dynasty tomb discovered on the slopes of Huang-wen Mountain, 15 kilometers south of Wu-hsing hsien, are most worthy of note. The excavation report says of these pieces, "The paste is a bluish purple color, and the mouth-rim and ring-foot are of the same color. The paste is firm and fine, similar to the Wu-ni ware type of southern Sung Kuan ware. The rim is in the shape of a six-petalled lotus blossom. . . . There is also a handled cup of light-blue color, with light blue glaze and crackling resembling ice-cracks. The ring-foot and mouth-rim are both reddish-purple in color, similar to what is commonly called the 'purple-mouth iron-foot' effect. The outer angle of the elbow-bend of the handle has a dry white color, due to the downward dripping of the glaze. . . . These three pieces should be classified as Sung dynasty Kuan ware." The three pieces in question are all beautifully made, with the same elegant Sung stylistic characteristics of the other burial pieces in this tomb. The single-handled cup is similar to a Chün-glazed round-bottomed single-handled cup in the National Palace Museum collection. The tomb cup has a dry white appearance on the handle, due to the dripping of the glaze from the off-white paste, and at the bend the paste gives off a bluish-white color, an effect sometimes called "Revealing the Tendon." This is all characteristic of Lung-ch'üan ware. Thus, although the "purple-mouth iron-foot" effect is found on this cup, it should be considered a Lung-ch'üan imitation of Kuan ware. The two celadon lotus-petal bowls are reported to have rims and ring-feet of the same color as their paste, which is to say they are unglazed at the mouth-rim and ring-foot. This tomb has been dated to the late Northern or early Southern Sung period (c. 1126);

if this date is correct, these pieces would have come from just around the time the Emperor Hui-tsung had ordered the creation of Ju ware celadon, an act inspired by his disdain for the unglazed rims of Ting ware. How could such elegant and exemplary unglazed-rim celadon works as these have been made in this period, when precisely the unglazed rim had been censured by imperial decree, and thus such pieces should have been at their lowest ebb? This is difficult to understand. But are these pieces then Southern Sung Kuan ware? Was there perhaps some difference in the manufacture of pieces intended for presentation as tribute at court and those not so intended? Or were these pieces made especially for use as burial objects? At present we have no answers to these questions; but the problem is made even more puzzling by the fact that the earliest date of Lung-ch'üan imitation Kuan ware is commonly believed to have been almost 75 years later than this tomb was sealed, as indicated in Chu Po-ch'ien's article "On Southern Sung Kuan Ware" ("T'an Nan-Sung Kuan-yao," 談南宋官窯 ), which states, "The Lung-ch'üan kiln probably began to make its thick-glazed imitations of Kuan ware around the year 1200." It is to be hoped that future research into the date of this tomb and the location of the kiln-site will shed further light on these problems.

All of the above cited examples come from Chekiang province. Elsewhere, in An-ch'ing city of Anhui province, a storage cave was discovered containing eight porcelain pieces arranged inside a large earthenware jar. Five of these were celadon ware, of which the excavation report stated, "All were unglazed on the bottom of the ring-foot, giving an iron-black color, and thinly glazed on the mouth-rim, giving a deep purple color." Another of the pieces found in this jar, a greyish yellow glazed dish, was evidently fired with six supports on the inside of the ring-foot; the report identifies it as "a Yüan dynasty imitation of Southern Sung Kuan ware, made at Ching-te-chen." The form of this piece is similar to that of pieces #118-121 in this exhibit, with glaze covering the entire surface of the support-fired bottom, but the mouth-rims of the Museum pieces are shaped like mallow flowers, and two of them have such extreme glaze-flow effects that they almost appear to have a layer of copper applied to their rims. A greyish-yellow handled cup from this cave is similar to piece #75 in this exhibit, except that it is somewhat larger and the glaze material is a bit denser, giving the cave piece a thicker, heavier feel. A set of pieces consisting of a Yüan dynasty mallow-flower shaped underglaze blue plate and basin were found together with this cup. The above-mentioned celadon plate has relatively flat and even walls and an everted rim, a style commonly seen on Yüan dynasty pieces. The glaze style however seems to fall somewhere between the glaze types usually found on Kuan ware and on Ko ware; it is possible that during this period of the Yüan dynasty very similar types of glaze were used on some imitations of Kuan and Ko ware, perhaps leading to the later practice of classifying the two as variants types of a single ware.

Also worthy of attention in this connection are the 11 mallow-shaped celadon plates of various sizes discovered at the early Ming (1371) tomb of Wang Hsing-tsu, forming a set with a number of Yüan underglaze blue pieces. These pieces are identified by the Nanking Municipal Museum's excavation report as Ko ware. The middle-sized plates resemble piece #79 in this exhibit, while the small ones resemble piece #119, even in the crackling effect of the glaze, which gives off a slight bluish color. These pieces, although found in an early Ming tomb, are probably of Yüan manufacture.

We should also take notice of a celadon gall-bladder vase with a fish-handled burner discovered in the Jen-shih family tombs in Shanghai, Ch'ing-p'u hsien; the form of the burner closely resembles that of piece #36. The latter burner has a dense and heavy glaze, with a glaze-flow effect used to thin the glaze at the mouth-rim, giving the purple rim effect. This is indubitably a late Southern Sung or Yüan glaze, and this piece can in fact be used as a reference for understanding how imitation of the Kuan-style glaze was handled during the Yüan. The gall-bladder vase, however, has been identified as a Sung dynasty product by Wang Ch'ing-cheng. The gall-bladder vase identified in this exhibit as piece #45 has a thin, glossy glaze and a strictly regular form to it; the glaze has a consistency like that of a Kuan ware vase with everted rim in the Percival David collection, although the David piece has somewhat richer lines to its form.

All of the above pieces, with the possible exception of the Shanghai gall-bladder vase, the two lotus-shaped plates from the Sung tomb on Huang-wen Mountain in Wu-hsing, Chekiang province, and the light-blue handled cup, are of the finest quality material and are exquisitely made, but whether or not they are Southern Sung Kuan ware is still difficult to determine. Indeed, at present no definite examples of fine Southern Sung Kuan ware used as burial objects have been found (the contents of the Sung imperial tombs being as yet unknown), which further underscores the uniqueness of Kuan ware: it would seem that people did not want to waste such exquisite pieces by burying them with the dead, so lesser wares were used in their place. This high esteem is no doubt not unrelated to the popularity of this ware with later collectors and the appearance of skillful imitators in the Yüan, Ming and Ch'ing dynasties. A significant portion of the pieces in the National Palace Museum currently catalogued as Sung Kuan ware are in reality clearly Ch'ing dynasty products, as can be seen from their glazes and pastes, and their neat and even ring-feet with rounded bottoms (i.e. the rim surface which touches the ground is rounded rather than squared and flat), all of which are characteristic of Ch'ing styles. This is especially evident in the pieces with inscriptions by the Ch'ien-lung Emperor, for example the matched sets of pieces #46 and #47, and #48 and #49, which, although differing somewhat in glaze-color and design of the bottom, are all marked by their characteristic Ch'ing paste and glaze materials. The glaze on the two identical tri-level *fang-hu* shaped square vases is rather dense, unlike that on Southern Sung Kuan ware; the rounded bottoms of the ring-feet are especially unlike Kuan ware. One of the pieces has a Ch'ien-lung inscription on the bottom, while the other in uninscribed. There is another tri-level *fang-hu* shaped square vase in the National Palace Museum collection, somewhat more sloppily constructed and not included in this exhibit, with a glaze like that on piece #5. The bottom of the stratified ring-foot on piece #1 is exceptionally neat and even, and the border between the glaze and the paste is also extremely neat. This type of ring-foot construction first appeared in the K'ang-hsi period (1662-1722), and is characterized by a thin and even coat of glaze and fine, delicate crackles. This gives the near-transparent glaze a rather unnatural and dull appearance. A light brown coloring (possibly some kind of glue) was applied to the mouth-rim after firing, to deliberately create the purple-mouth effect. Examples of this type of thin, near-transparent celadon glazing, made glossy by special polishing, can be seen on the *li*-shaped burner displayed as piece #31, the octagonal dish displayed as piece #76, the narcissus pot displayed as piece #43 and the portable vase with dish-shaped mouth displayed as piece #26. All these pieces except the narcissus pot have an unglazed ring-foot bottom onto which a layer of iron paint has been applied, giving the iron-foot effect. All the measurements of the narcissus pot are akin to those of the Ju ware narcissus pots in the National Palace Museum collection, as are the support traces on its bottom. These support traces appear at first glance to have a brown color, but upon close examination with magnification, it is clear that the dark brown coloring of these traces was applied to them after firing, and that the original paste was off-white in color. Piece #26 closely resembles piece #25 in its form and measurements, except that the glaze on the latter is thick and glossy, with large colored crackles. The bottom of the ring-foot of piece #26 is rounded and colored with a layer of iron paint, giving it a dark, glossy appearance. The same effect is seen on piece #25, the glaze and ring-foot design of which are typical of Ch'ing dynasty Yung-cheng and Ch'ien-lung period (1723-1795) imitations of Ju and Kuan ware. The two pieces differ drastically in glaze material and in weight, but X-rays show that their internal structure of joins is identical: both are constructed of three pieces, assembled by one join at the belly and one in the neck. From these two pieces we can see the care and attention devoted to imitating the paste and glaze of Kuan ware in the Yung-cheng and Ch'ien-lung periods. Of all the portable vases with dish-shaped mouths and hoop-decor, the most natural glaze effect is to be found on piece #22, but a careful examination of the unglazed part of the ring-foot reveals that the iron-foot effect is obtained by the application of a layer of dark brown coloring to the bottom, and moreover, the ring-foot itself is made unevenly. Additional doubt is cast on this piece by its heavy paste, and the indentation that appears between the inner flat of the ring-foot and the body of the vessel, all of which is typical of porcelain made by the imperial workshops during the Yung-cheng and Ch'ien-lung periods. Thus the accuracy of a Sung dating for this group of dish-shaped mouth vases is extremely doubtful.

The joins in the bottom of piece #18 are extremely unusual, extending the octagonal shape clear through to the ground and then attaching another disk of porcelain to form the ring-foot bottom; in other words, the piece seems to have been assembled from two main parts, an octagonal tube and a flat plate. It might seem at first that this method was designed to accomodate the octagonal shape, but piece #12 is ovular and not octagonal, and yet it's bottom is also constructed in this way. The vessel bottoms of these two pieces are both indented, and their dense glazes are also similar. In both cases the unglazed bottom of the ring-foot has a shallow layer of dark brown and the glaze-flow at the rim is quite obvious but not to the extent of revealing the paste and creating the purple-mouth effect. Other pieces of this general shape, such as #9 and #10, although also ovular, nonetheless have bottoms which are of one piece with the main body of the vessel, giving a smooth and even appearance. The glaze and paste materials of these two pieces are typical of Southern Sung Kuan ware, which further underscores the uniqueness of the structure of pieces #12 and #18. There is another piece of the same construction in this exhibit, the octagonal vase displayed as piece #53. The same type of glaze is used on all three pieces, which, together with the deliberate determination to create a particular appearance evidenced by this unusual use of a separately made bottom, suggests that they are imitations made one by one on an ad hoc basis in unusual conditions, sometime after the discontinuation of Southern Sung Kuan ware. The type of glaze used is relatively dense, similar to that on a *kuei*-shaped burner found in one of the Yüan dynasty Jen-shih tombs in Shanghai, but with more impurities. Since the appearance of the ring-foot is quite natural, with no deliberate application of a "paste-protective glaze" (coloring) or special polishing to enhance its shine, this piece probably dates from no later than the Ch'ing dynasty. The formal design of piece #13, a *fang-hu* shaped square vase with almond decor, did not appear until the Ch'ing dynasty; this piece is quite heavy, with an extremely neat and even ring-foot and a very glossy shine to the glaze. The glaze and paste of piece #11, a loop-earred portable *fang-hu* shaped square vase, are of the same type as those of piece #25, but the lines of the form, although symmetrical and even, are excessively sharp and angular, unlike those characteristic of Sung dynasty works.

All the mallow-petal brush washers in this exhibit were propped up on six supports during firing. They show a certain diversity of design, however, in that some of the mouth-rims have eight petals, some nine and some ten; in addition, each is glazed differently. There may also be a significant variance in date of manufacture between them. The case of the mallow-shaped plates in the exhibit differs somewhat, in that some were fired on supports while others have ring-feet. The former are perhaps the earlier of the two types, but it is clear from their glaze and forms that both types are post-Southern Sung products; this is clear from the close resemblence of pieces #79 and #119 to the dish from the Ming dynasty tomb of Wang Hsing-tsu discussed above. Further, we can take as an example piece #38, an extremely interesting celadon work, with a thick paste and glaze and an exceptionially heavy body. There are large crackles in the glaze and a dark brown color to the exposed paste on the ring-foot, an iron-foot effect created by adding coloring. Five protruding conical supports appear inside the bottom of the ring-foot, smooth and glossy but unglazed, and also dark brown in color. There is coloring in the crackle designs, an effect found mostly on the non-Southern-Sung pieces in this exhibit. Two characters, written in unglazed relief, appear on the bottom; the top one appears to be *chung,* the bottom one *ch'eng,* which together mean Vice Censor-in-chief. Perhaps this is related to Lang T'ing-chi's supervision of the Ching-te-chen imperial kiln while he was Provincial Governor of Kiangsi during the K'ang-hsi period; his friend Hsü Chin-chai said in a poem, "In the year kuei-chi, I went down to Lang's kiln to enjoy his company, to see old Vice Censor-in-chief Tzu-heng [Lang's sobriquet]." The form of this burner is similar to that of a K'ang-hsi period copper-bodied enamel burner with ice-crackle and plum-blossom decor in the National Palace Museum collection, and is often found on K'ang-hsi underglaze blue burners. Piece

#38 appears to have been made by a craftsman who was attempting to imitate Sung Kuan ware purely on the basis of written descriptions of its features without ever having seen an actual specimen; it was enough to create a porcelain object with thick glaze, a purple-mouth, an iron-foot effect and fired on supports. And yet this piece, by very virtue of the inadvertant inaccuracies of this inefficient method of imitation, is actually quite fascinating and attractive.

Many of the pieces classified as Sung Kuan ware in the National Palace Museum can be judged, on the basis of some of the more distinctive pieces among them, and from their glaze, paste, form and manufacture, to be imitations made in the Yüan, Ming and Ch'ing dynasties, and this in turn gives us a better understanding of all the pieces in the collection. Some of these works are easily classifiable, having fairly obvious and easily distinguished characteristics, while others are somewhat more difficult to differentiate. The works of the late Southern Sung and Yüan dynasty are especially difficult to distinguish, since the fluctuations which occurred at the kilns over the 150 or so years of the Southern Sung in accord with the changing times are impossible to know with any certainty. We might perhaps infer from these pieces that the quality of Kuan ware production had already begun to decline even before the advent of the Yüan dynasty, but the truth of this inference, and how extensive such decline might have been, cannot be determined until reports of the excavation of the Hangchow kiln-site are made public.

This special exhibition of Sung Kuan ware illustrates that the number of top-grade pieces of Kuan ware made, even during its peak of prosperity, are fewer than might have been imagined. A great many later imitations have been erroneously identified as Sung Kuan ware, due to the guesses and unreliable classifications put forth during the fad for porcelain research among amateur bourgeois scholars in the post Ch'ien-lung periods of the Ch'ing dynasty; the vast quantity of imitations and the lack of historical materials from the Yüan and Ming made such errors almost inevitable. This is a natural result of the limitations of knowledge in any given historical period. However, the assemblage of celadon pieces gathered together in the National Palace Museum under this heading provides an excellent source of materials for further research. It is hoped that in the future the expert guidance of skillful scholars will lead us to a more accurate understanding of the true history of Sung Kuan ware.

# 圖版目錄

| | | |
|---|---|---|
| 37. 宋　哥窯米邑三足圓爐 | 7 | 崑二二八 74 |
| 38. 清　仿官釉青瓷圓爐 | 201 | 闕四二九 72 |
| 39. 南宋　脩內司官窯粉青缽（匏） | 556 | T2014 |
| 40. 南宋　脩內司官窯粉青缽 | 416 | T3803 |
| 41. 南宋　脩內司官窯灰青缽 | 1768 | JW94 |
| 42. 南宋　郊壇下官窯渣斗 | 1101 | JW96 |
| 43. 北宋　官窯天青橢圓水仙盆 | 5 | 呂一八四六 62之1 |
| 44. 南宋　脩內司官窯粉青長方盆 | 35 | 雨五六八 |
| 45. 北宋　官窯粉青膽瓶 | 4 | 呂一八○四 34 |
| 46. 北宋　官窯粉青弦紋瓶 | 1729 | 金二○四三 |
| 47. 北宋　官窯粉青弦紋瓶 | 140 | JW1474 |
| 48. 北宋　官窯粉青花挿 | 1697 | 珍二四九 7 |
| 49. 北宋　官窯粉青花挿 | 5 | 呂一八四七 72 |
| 50. 南宋　脩內司官窯粉青花挿 | 152 | 呂一七九○ 54 |
| 51. 南宋　脩內司官窯淺粉青花挿 | 224 | 金一九八三 |
| 52. 南宋　郊壇下官窯灰青海棠式花挿 | 2403 | 出二二七 19 |
| 53. 南宋　脩內司官窯月白凹稜膽瓶 | 8 | 呂一八○四 10 |
| 54. 南宋　郊壇下官窯月白海棠式貫耳瓶 | 11 | 呂一八○四 5 |
| 55. 南宋　郊壇下官窯粉青海棠式小瓶 | 11 | 呂一八○四 8 |
| 56. 南宋　郊壇下官窯灰青葫蘆瓶 | 269 | JW130 |
| 57. 南宋　脩內司官窯月白葫蘆瓶 | 8 | 金二八一 37 |
| 58. 南宋　脩內司官窯粉青葵花式洗 | 35 | 雨四八五 |
| 59. 南宋　脩內司官窯月白雙蓮房水注 | 5 | 崑二二七 6 |
| 60. 北宋　官窯天青臂擱 | 5 | 呂一七九○ 25 |
| 61. 北宋　官窯月白小水注 | 5 | 呂一七九○ 56之2 |
| 62. 北宋　官窯粉青筆筒 | 5 | 呂一七九○ 82 |
| 63. 南宋　脩內司官窯淺青橢圓硯 | 1748 | 天一一三七 |
| 64. 南宋　脩內司官窯月白葵花式水盛 | 1829 | 為四九一 5 |
| 65. 清　仿官釉筆架 | 224 | 闕五○一 25 |
| 66. 南宋　郊壇下官窯天青葉式洗 | 164 | 藏一二六 47 |
| 67. 北宋　官窯粉青葵花式小盌 | 152 | 呂一七九○ 12之2 |
| 68. 北宋　官窯粉青葵花式小盌 | 152 | 呂一七九○ 12之1 |
| 69. 清　乾隆仿官釉葵花口盌 | 1514 | 藏四七○ 之1 |
| 70. 北宋　官窯粉青梅花式栖 | 1748 | 天一一三三 |
| 71. 北宋　官窯天青菱花式小盌 | 5 | 呂一七九○ 96 |
| 72. 北宋　官窯粉青蓮花式花挿 | 260 | 呂一七九○ 76 |

| | | | | |
|---|---|---|---|---|
| 73. | 南宋 | 郊壇下官窯灰青牡丹花式栮 | 2287 | 金七八 1之2 |
| 74. | 南宋 | 脩內司官窯粉青八方栮 | 152 | 呂一七九〇 51 |
| 75. | 南宋 | 脩內司官窯粉青把栮 | 2287 | 金七八 11 |
| 76. | 北宋 | 官窯月白八方盤 | 33 | 闞四二九 55 |
| 77. | 南宋 | 脩內司官窯月白葵口碟 | 164 | 闞四三〇 76 |
| 78. | 南宋 | 脩內司官窯灰青劃花蟠龍碟 | 32 | 闞四三〇 102 |
| 79. | 南宋 | 郊壇下官窯灰青葵口碟 | 2906 | JW150 |
| 80. | 南宋 | 脩內司官窯粉青圓洗 | 8 | 闞四三〇 112 |
| 81. | 南宋 | 郊壇下官窯圓洗 | 1874 | JW129 |
| 82. | 南宋 | 脩內司官窯粉青彫龍圓洗 | 32 | 金二四七 51之1 |
| 83. | 南宋 | 脩內司官窯粉青大圓洗 | 230 | 呂一九三二 |
| 84. | 南宋 | 郊壇下官窯灰青葵瓣口小洗 | 191 | 麗一一九三 3 |
| 85. | 南宋 | 脩內司官窯粉青蔗段圓洗 | 8 | 闞四二九 49 |
| 86. | 南宋 | 脩內司官窯淺青葵瓣口洗 | 262 | 呂一八四六 19 |
| 87. | 南宋 | 脩內司官窯粉青葵瓣口洗 | 33 | 崑一六一 3 |
| 88. | 南宋 | 脩內司官窯粉青大圓盤 | 32 | 金二八〇 70之3 |
| 89. | 南宋 | 郊壇下官窯灰青大圓盤 | 1765 | JW163 |
| 90. | 南宋 | 脩內司官窯粉青大圓盤 | 7 | 闞五〇一 11 |
| 91. | 南宋 | 郊壇下官窯粉青葵瓣口龍紋盤 | 548 | T2487 |
| 92. | 南宋 | 脩內司官窯粉青菱花式盤 | 33 | 崑二二八 41 |
| 93. | 南宋 | 脩內司官窯粉青蓮花式盤 | 33 | 金二〇五六 |
| 94. | 南宋 | 脩內司官窯青牡丹花式盤 | 8 | 麗一〇五八 14之2 |
| 95. | 南宋 | 郊壇下官窯粉青菊花式盤 | 1092 | JW162 |
| 96. | 南宋 | 脩內司官窯粉青蓮瓣盤 | 196 | 闞四三〇 20之7 |
| 97. | 南宋 | 脩內司官窯天青蓮瓣盤 | 191 | 奈三九六 25 |
| 98. | 南宋 | 脩內司官窯粉青葵花式盤 | 136 | 麗一一二九 3之15 |
| 99. | 南宋 | 脩內司官窯翠青葵花式盤 | 185 | 亘一八一 29 |
| 100. | 南宋 | 脩內司官窯粉青葵花式盤 | 7 | 麗一〇五八 14之1 |
| 101. | 南宋 | 脩內司官窯粉青葵花式盤 | 7 | 金二八〇 70之2 |
| 102. | 南宋 | 脩內司官窯青葵花式盤 | 196 | 闞五〇一 12 |
| 103. | 南宋 | 脩內司官窯天青葵花式盤 | 1615 | 珍四五 之1 |
| 104. | 南宋 | 脩內司官窯粉青葵花式淺盌 | 196 | 闞四三〇 122 |
| 105. | 南宋 | 脩內司官窯粉青葵花式盌 | 8 | 闞四三〇 50 |
| 106. | 南宋 | 郊壇下官窯灰青葵花式盌 | 33 | 麗一〇五七 6 |
| 107. | 南宋 | 脩內司官窯粉青葵花式大盌 | 136 | 徍一四八 30之2 |
| 108. | 南宋 | 脩內司官窯月白大盌 | 146 | 闞四三〇 65 |

| | | |
|---|---|---|
| 109. 南宋　脩內司官窯粉青葵口大盌 | 2906 | JW160 |
| 110. 南宋　脩內司官窯粉青菊瓣盌 | 196 | 律一四八 29之2 |
| 111. 宋　龍泉窯天青蓮瓣盌 | 191 | 律一四七 15之1 |
| 112. 宋　龍泉窯粉青盌 | 191 | 律一四八 4 |
| 113. 南宋　脩內司官窯粉青盌 | 210 | 闕四三〇 42 |
| 114. 南宋　郊壇下官窯粉青葵瓣口盌 | 224 | 律一四八 17之2 |
| 115. 南宋　脩內司官窯粉青盌 | 152 | 呂一七九〇 40之2 |
| 116. 南宋　郊壇下官窯粉青葵瓣口盌 | 1697 | 珍二四九 3 |
| 117. 宋　龍泉窯翠青盌 | 1697 | 珍二四九 5 |
| 118. 南宋　郊壇下官窯灰青葵瓣口碟 | 224 | 麗一一二九 3之8 |
| 119. 南宋　郊壇下官窯灰青葵瓣口碟 | 146 | 麗一一二九 3之9 |
| 120. 南宋　郊壇下官窯灰青葵瓣口碟 | 1644 | 闕四三〇 94之1 |
| 121. 南宋　脩內司官窯淺青葵瓣口碟 | 196 | 律一四八 14之1 |
| 122. 南宋　郊壇下官窯月白葵瓣口碟 | 1670 | 麗一〇七六 2 |
| 123. 南宋　脩內司官窯月白葵瓣口碟 | 1729 | 金一九八二 1 |
| 124. 南宋　脩內司官窯月白葵瓣口碟 | 1768 | JW95 |
| 125. 南宋　脩內司官窯月白葵瓣口碟 | 7 | 麗一一二九 3之12 |
| 126. 南宋　脩內司官窯淺青葵瓣口碟 | 223 | 珍二〇〇 之12 |
| 127. 南宋　脩內司官窯灰青葵瓣口碟 | 276 | JW97 |
| 128. 南宋　脩內司官窯月白葵瓣口碟 | 1644 | 闕四三〇 20之2 |
| 129. 南宋　脩內司官窯月白葵瓣口碟 | 7 | 麗一一二九 3之11 |
| 130. 南宋　脩內司官窯月白葵瓣口碟 | 1644 | 闕四三〇 20之3 |
| 131. 南宋　脩內司官窯月白葵瓣口碟 | 164 | 闕四三〇 83 |
| 132. 南宋　郊壇下官窯灰青菊瓣口碟 | 1644 | 闕四三〇 74 |
| 133. 南宋　郊壇下官窯灰青菊瓣口碟 | 201 | 麗一一二九 3之2 |
| 134. 南宋　郊壇下官窯粉青葵瓣口碟 | 201 | 麗一一二九 3之3 |
| 135. 南宋　脩內司官窯月白牡丹花式洗 | 201 | 麗一一二九 3之16 |
| 136. 南宋　脩內司官窯月白牡丹花式洗 | 224 | 麗一六五八 |
| 137. 南宋　脩內司官窯粉青牡丹花式洗 | 1510 | 菜四七九 14 |
| 138. 南宋　郊壇下官窯灰青牡丹花式洗 | 224 | 闕四三〇 52 |
| 139. 南宋　郊壇下官窯粉青牡丹花式洗 | 196 | 崑二二六 6 |
| 140. 南宋　脩內司官窯淺青牡丹花式洗 | 224 | 闕四二九 66之2 |
| 141. 南宋　郊壇下官窯灰青牡丹花式洗 | 164 | 崑二二八 65 |
| 142. 南宋　郊壇下官窯灰青牡丹花式洗 | 1768 | JW92 |
| 143. 南宋　脩內司官粉青牡丹花式洗 | 1670 | 麗一一二九 3之26 |

# List of Plates

1. Flower receptacle in the form of a bronze *ku*
   Kuan ware
2. Vase in the form of a bronze *tsun*
   Hsiu-nei-ssu Kuan ware
3. Pyramidal vase with a three-terraced body
   Kuan ware
4. Pyramidal vase with a three-terraced body
   Kúan ware
5. Vase in the form of a bronze *hu*, Kuan ware
6. Two-handled flask, Kuan ware
7. Small angular vase in the form of a bronze *hu*
   Kuan ware
8. Vase in the form of a bronze *hu* with hooped
   decor, Hsiu-nei-ssu Kuan ware
9. Vase in the form of a bronze *hu*
   Hsiu-nei-ssu Kuan ware
10. Vase in the shape of a bronze *hu* with hooped
    decor, Hsiu-nei-ssu Kuan ware
11. Angular vase in the shape of a bronze *hu*
    Hsiu-nei-ssu Kuan ware
12. Vase in the shape of a bronze *hu*
    Hsiu-nei-ssu Kuan ware
13. Angular vase in the form of a bronze *hu* with
    relief apricot leaf decor
    Hsiu-nei-ssu Kuan ware
14. Vase with hooped decoration
    Hsiu-nei-ssu Kuan ware
15. Octagonal vase with tubular handles
    Hsiu-nei-ssu Kuan ware
16. Octagonal vase with tubular handles
    Chiao-t'an-hsia Kuan ware
17. Vase in the form of a bronze *hu* with vertical
    flange decor, Chiao-t'an-hsia Kuan ware
18. Octagonal vase with tubular handles
    Chiao-t'an-hsia Kuan ware
19. Vase with two tubular handles
    Hsiu-nei-ssu Kuan ware
20. Vase with two tubular handles
    Hsiu-nei-ssu Kuan ware
21. Vase with hooped decoration
    Hsiu-nei-ssu Kuan ware
22. Vase with hooped decoration
    Hsiu-nei-ssu Kuan ware
23. Vase with hooped decoration
    Hsiu-nei-ssu Kuan ware
24. Small vase in the shape of a paper-mallet
    Hsiu-nei-ssu Kuan ware
25. Vase with hooped decoration
    Chiao-t'an-hsia Kuan ware
26. Vase with dish-like mouth and hooped
    decoration, Chiao-t'an-hsia Kuan ware
27. Vase with hooped decoration (date unknown)
28. Vase with flared mouth
    Chiao-t'an-hsia Kuan ware
29. Globular vase, Chiao-t'an-hsia Kuan ware
30. Vase with hooped decoration
    Hsiu-nei-ssu Kuan ware
31. Incense burner in the shape of a bronze *li*
    Kuan ware
32. Tripodal incense burner with two handles
    Kuan ware
33. Tripodal incense burner with two handles
    Kuan ware
34. Round tripodal incense burner, Kuan ware
35. Incense burner in the shape of a bronze *kuei*
    with hooped decorations
    Hsiu-nei-ssu Kuan ware
36. Small incense burner in the shape of a bronze
    *kuei*, Chiao-t'an-hsia Kuan ware
37. Round tripodal incense burner, Ko ware
38. Imitation of Kuan glazed incense burner
39. Almsbowl, Hsiu-nei-ssu Kuan ware
40. Almsbowl, Hsiu-nei-ssu Kuan ware
41. Almsbowl, Hsiu-nei-ssu Kuan ware

42. Spittoon, Chiao-t'an-hsia Kuan ware
43. Oval narcissus pot, Kuan ware
44. Rectangular pot, Hsiu-nei-ssu Kuan ware
45. Vase in the shape of a gall-bladder, Kuan ware
46. Vase with hooped decoration, Kuan ware
47. Vase with hooped decoration, Kuan ware
48. Flower receptacle, Kuan ware
49. Flower receptacle, Kuan ware
50. Flower receptacle, Hsiu-nei-ssu Kuan ware
51. Flower receptacle, Hsiu-nei-ssu Kuan ware
52. Flower receptacle with begonia-shaped rim
    Chiao-t'an-hsia Kuan ware
53. Gall-bladder shaped vase with fluted corners
    Hsiu-nei-ssu Kuan ware
54. Vase with tubular handles and begonia-shaped rim, Chiao-t'an-hsia Kuan ware
55. Small vase with begonia-shaped rim
    Chiao-t'an-hsia Kuan ware
56. Gourd-shaped vase
57. Gourd-shaped vase
58. Hibiscus-shaped brush-washer
59. Double lotus-pod shaped water dropper
    Hsiu-nei-ssu Kuan ware
60. Armrest, Kuan ware
61. Small water dropper, Kuan ware
62. Brush holder, Kuan ware
63. Oval inkstone, Hsiu-nei-ssu Kuan ware
64. Floral-shaped water container
    Hsiu-nei-ssu Kuan ware
65. Brush stand with imitation Kuan glaze
66. Leaf-shaped brush washer
    Chiao-t'an-hsia Kuan ware
67. Small floral-shaped bowl, Kuan ware
68. Small floral-shaped bowl, Kuan ware
69. Bowl with foliated rim, Ch'ien-lung period
    (1736-1795) imitation of Kuan ware
70. Plum blossom-shaped cup, Kuan ware

71. Small floral-shaped bowl, Kuan ware
72. Lotus-shaped flower receptacle, Kuan ware
73. Cup with peony-shaped rim
    Chiao-t'an-hsia Kuan ware
74. Octagonal cup, Hsiu-nei-ssu Kuan ware
75. Cup with handle, Hsiu-nei-ssu Kuan ware
76. Octagonal dish, Kuan ware
77. Dish with hibiscus petal rim
    Hsiu-nei-ssu Kuan ware
78. Dish with incised coiled dragon design
    Hsiu-nei-ssu Kuan ware
79. Dish with foliated petal rim
    Chiao-t'an-hsia Kuan ware
80. Round basin, Hsiu-nei-ssu Kuan ware
81. Round basin, Chiao-t'an-hsia Kuan ware
82. Round basin with dragon design in relief
    Hsiu-nei-ssu Kuan ware
83. Round large basin, Hsiu-nei-ssu Kuan ware
84. Small basin with foliated rim
    Chiao-t'an-hsia Kuan ware
85. Round basin with cut sugarcane design
    Hsiu-nei-ssu Kuan ware
86. Basin with foliated rim
    Hsiu-nei-ssu Kuan ware
87. Basin with foliated rim
    Hsiu-nei-ssu Kuan ware
88. Large round dish, Hsiu-nei-ssu Kuan ware
89. Large round dish, Chiao-t'an-hsia Kuan ware
90. Round dish, Hsiu-nei-ssu Kuan ware
91. Dish with foliated rim and dragon decor
    Chiao-t'an-hsia Kuan ware
92. Lobed dish with foliated rim
    Hsiu-nei-ssu Kuan ware
93. Lobed disk with foliated rim
    Hsiu-nei-ssu Kuan ware
94. Lobed dish with foliated rim
    Hsiu-nei-ssu Kuan ware

95. Chrysanthemum-shaped dish
Chiao-t'an-hsia Kuan ware
96. Lobed dish with foliated rim
Hsiu-nei-ssu Kuan ware
97. Dish with lotus petal shaped lobes
Hsiu-nei-ssu Kuan ware
98. Dish with foliated rim
Hsiu-nei-ssu Kuan ware
99. Dish with foliated rim, Hsiu-nei-ssu Kuan ware
100. Dish with foliated rim, Hsiu-nei-ssu Kuan ware
101. Dish with foliated rim, Hsiu-nei-ssu Kuan ware
102. Dish with foliated rim, Hsiu-nei-ssu Kuan ware
103. Dish with foliated rim, Hsiu-nei-ssu Kuan ware
104. Shallow bowl with foliated rim
Hsiu-nei-ssu Kuan ware
105. Bowl with foliated rim
Hsiu-nei-ssu Kuan ware
106. Bowl with foliated rim
Chiao-t'an-hsia Kuan ware
107. Large bowl with foliated rim
Hsiu-nei-ssu Kuan ware
108. Large bowl, Hsiu-nei-ssu Kuan ware
109. Large bowl with foliated rim
Hsiu-nei-ssu Kuan ware
110. Bowl with moulded chrysanthemum petal
shaped lobes, Hsiu-nei-ssu Kuan ware
111. Bowl with lotus petal shaped lobes
Lung-ch'uan ware
112. Hat-shaped bowl, Lung-ch'üan ware
113. Small shallow bowl, Hsiu-nei-ssu Kuan ware
114. Small shallow bowl with foliated rim
Chiao-t'an-hsia Kuan ware
115. Small shallow bowl, Hsiu-nei-ssu Kuan ware
116. Small shallow bowl with foliated rim
Chiao-t'an-hsia Kuan ware
117. Small shallow bowl, Lung-ch'üan ware
118. Dish with foliated rim
Chiao-t'an-hsia Kuan ware

119. Dish with foliated rim
Chiao-t'an-hsia Kuan ware
120. Dish with foliated rim
Chiao-t'an-hsia Kuan ware
121. Dish with foliated rim, Hsiu-nei-ssu Kuan ware
122. Dish with foliated rim
Chiao-t'an-hsia Kuan ware
123. Dish with foliated rim, Hsiu-nei-ssu Kuan ware
124. Dish with foliated rim, Hsiu-nei-ssu Kuan ware
125. Dish with foliated rim, Hsiu-nei-ssu Kuan ware
126. Dish with foliated rim, Hsiu-nei-ssu Kuan ware
127. Dish with foliated rim, Hsiu-nei-ssu Kuan ware
128. Dish with foliated rim, Hsiu-nei-ssu Kuan ware
129. Dish with foliated rim, Hsiu-nei-ssu Kuan ware
130. Dish with foliated rim, Hsiu-nei-ssu Kuan ware
131. Dish with foliated rim, Hsiu-nei-ssu Kuan ware
132. Dish with foliated rim, Hsiu-nei-ssu Kuan ware
133. Dish with foliated rim, Hsiu-nei-ssu Kuan ware
134. Dish with foliated rim, Hsiu-nei-ssu Kuan ware
135. Floral-shaped basin, Hsiu-nei-ssu Kuan ware
136. Floral-shaped basin, Hsiu-nei-ssu Kuan ware
137. Floral-shaped basin, Hsiu-nei-ssu Kuan ware
138. Floral-shaped basin, Hsiu-nei-ssu Kuan ware
139. Floral-shaped basin, Hsiu-nei-ssu Kuan ware
140. Floral-shaped basin, Hsiu-nei-ssu Kuan ware
141. Floral-shaped basin, Hsiu-nei-ssu Kuan ware
142. Floral-shaped basin, Hsiu-nei-ssu Kuan ware
143. Floral-shaped basin, Hsiu-nei-ssu Kuan ware

圖

版
PLATES

1. 北宋　官窯粉青花觚
　高17.8公分　口徑15.0公分　深16.2公分　足徑5.5公分
　崑二二六[18]
Flower receptacle in the form of a bronze *ku*
Kuan ware

2. 南宋　脩內司官窯粉青尊
　　高25.9公分　口徑16.5公分　深24.1公分
　　足徑13.0公分　雨五四七
Vase in the form of a bronze *tsun*
Hsiu-nei-ssu Kuan ware

3. 北宋　官窯粉青三登方壺
　　高12.2公分　口徑6.7×3.8公分　深10.0公分　底徑10.2×7.3公分
　　呂一八四七 31
　　Pyramidal vase with a three-terraced body
　　Kuan ware, Northern Sung Dynasty, 960-1126
　　Height: 12.2cm　　　Depth: 10.0cm
　　Mouth dimensions: 6.7 x 3.8cm　　　Base dimensions: 10.2 x 7.3cm

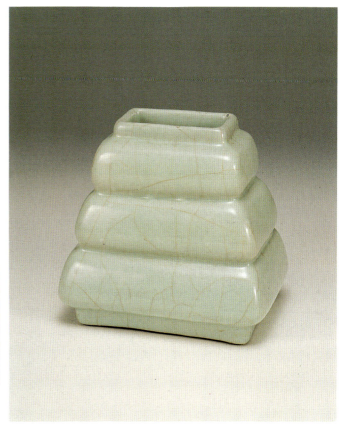

4. 北宋　官窯粉青三登方壺
　　高11.9公分　6.5×3.7公分　深10.0公分　底徑6.8×9.7公分
　　呂二八六
　　Pyramidal vase with a three-terraced body
　　Kuan ware, Northern Sung Dynasty, 960-1126
　　Height: 11.9cm　　　Depth: 10.0cm
　　Mouth dimensions: 6.5 x 3.7cm　　　Base dimensions: 9.7 x 6.8cm

5. 北宋　官窯月白貫耳弦紋壺
　　高14.6公分　口徑5.2×7.8公分　深13.2公分　足徑5.0×7.5公分
　　麗一〇五七 11
Vase in the form of a bronze *hu*
Kuan ware, Northern Sung Dynasty, 960-1126
Height: 14.6cm　　　Depth: 13.2cm
Mouth dimensions: 7.8 x 5.2cm　　　Base dimensions: 7.5 x 5.0cm

6. 北宋　官窯淺粉青弓耳扁壺
　　高11.8公分　口徑2.0公分　深11.2公分　足徑3.2×4.4公分
　　麗一〇八二
Two-handled flask
Kuan ware, Northern Sung Dynasty, 960-1126
Height: 11.8cm　　　Depth: 11.2cm
Mouth dimensions: 2.0cm　　　Base dimensions: 4.4 x 3.2cm

7. 北宋　官窯粉青貫耳穿帶小方壺
　　高8.4公分　口徑3.3×2.4公分　深7.4公分　足徑3.2×2.5公分
　　呂一七九〇 37
　　Small angular vase in the form of a bronze *hu*
　　Kuan ware, Northern Sung Dynasty, 960-1126
　　Height: 8.4cm　　　Depth: 7.4cm
　　Mouth dimensions: 3.3 x 2.4cm　　　Base dimensions: 3.2 x 2.5cm

8. 南宋　脩內司官窯粉青貫耳弦紋壺
　　高38.2公分　口徑14.2×18.3公分
　　深34.5公分　口徑14.2×19.3公分
　　足徑14.0×16.9公分　呂一九四〇

Vase in the form of a bronze *hu*
with hopped decor
Hsiu-nei-ssu Kuan ware,
Southern Sung Dynasty, 1127-1278
Height: 38.2cm　　　Depth: 34.5cm
Mouth dimensions: 18.3 x 14.2cm
Base dimensions: 14.0cm

9. 南宋　脩內司官窯粉青貫耳穿帶弦紋壺
高26.7公分　口徑11.1×9.5公分
深24.0公分　足徑10.3×12.0公分
雨五六六
Vase in the form of a bronze *hu*
Hsiu-nei-ssu Kuan ware,
Southern Sung Dynasty, 1127-1278
Height: 26.7cm　　Depth: 24.0cm
Mouth dimensions: 11.1 x 9.5cm
Base dimensions: 10.3 x 12.0cm

10. 南宋　脩內司官窯粉青貫耳弦紋方壺
　　高24.1公分　　口徑6.4×8.9公分
　　深21.9公分　　足徑9.2×11.0公分
　　棻四七七 11

Vase in the shape of a bronze *hu*
with hopped decor
Hsiu-nei-ssu Kuan ware,
Southern Sung Dynasty, 1127-1278
Height: 24.1 cm　　Depth: 21.9cm
Mouth dimensions: 8.9 x 6.4cm
Base dimensions: 11.0 x 9.2cm

11. 南宋　脩內司官窯粉青貫耳穿帶方壺
　　高21.0公分　口徑7×9.5公分　深18.9公分　足徑7.8×10.0公分
　　金二一二六

Angular vase in the shape of a bronze *hu*
Hsiu-nei-ssu Kuan ware, Southern Sung Dynasty, 1127-1278
Height: 21.0cm　　　Depth: 18.9cm
Mouth dimensions: 9.5 x 7.0cm　　　Base dimensions: 10.0 x 7.8cm

12. 南宋　脩內司官窯月白貫耳弦紋壺
　　高17.9公分　口徑5.7×7.2公分　深14.9公分　足徑6.8×7.7公分
　　雨八九一
Vase in the shape of a bronze *hu*
Hsiu-nei-ssu Kuan ware, Southern Sung Dynasty, 1127-1278
Height: 17.9cm　　　Depth: 14.9cm
Mouth dimensions: 7.2 x 5.7cm　　　Base dimensions: 7.7 x 6.8cm

13. 南宋　脩內司官窯粉青貫耳穿帶杏葉方壺
　　高17.3公分　口徑4.5×6.3公分　深15.8公分　足徑5.3×7.8公分
　　呂一三四6

Angular vase in the form of a bronze *hu* with relief apricot leaf decor
Hsiu-nei-ssu Kuan ware, Southern Sung Dynasty, 1127-1278
Height: 17.3cm　　Depth: 15.8cm
Mouth dimensions: 6.3 x 4.5cm　　Base dimensions: 7.8 x 5.3cm

14. 南宋　脩內司官窯粉青弦紋壺
　　高20.8公分　口徑10.2公分
　　深18.7公分　足徑11.6公分
　　JW 1466
　　Vase with hopped decoration
　　Hsiu-nei-ssu Kuan ware,
　　Southern Sung Dynasty, 1127-1278
　　Height: 20.8cm　　　Depth: 18.7cm
　　Mouth dimensions: 10.2cm
　　Base dimensions: 11.6cm

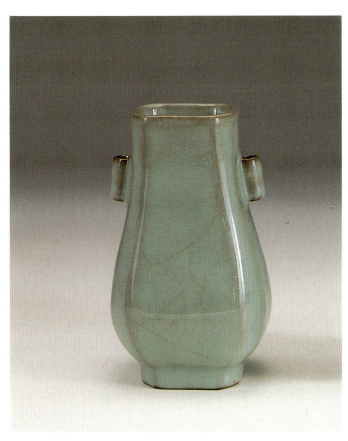

15. 南宋　脩內司官窯粉青貫耳八方壺
　　高14.0公分　口徑4.0×5.1公分　深12.7公分　足徑4.2×5.3公分
　　呂一八四六 30
　　Octagonal vase with tubular handles
　　Hsiu-nei-ssu Kuan ware, Southern Sung Dynasty, 1127-1278
　　Height: 14.0cm　　　Depth: 12.7cm
　　Mouth dimensions: 5.1 x 4.0cm　　　Base dimensions: 5.3 x 4.2cm

16. 南宋　郊壇下官窯月白貫耳穿帶八方壺
　　高15.1公分　口徑3.8×5.4公分　深13.6公分　足徑4.2×4.9公分
　　呂一八四六 66
　　Octagonal vase with tubular handles
　　Chiao-t'an-hsia Kuan ware, Southern Sung Dynasty, 1127-1278
　　Height: 15.1cm　　　Depth: 13.6cm
　　Mouth dimensions: 5.4 x 3.8cm　　　Base dimensions: 4.9 x 4.2cm

17. 南宋　郊壇下官窰粉青貫耳穿帶壺
　　高20.6公分　　口徑6.4×8.2公分
　　深18.2公分　　足徑7.5×8.9公分
　　雨九二四

Vase in the form of a bronze *hu*
with vertical flange decor
Chiao-t'an-hsia Kuan ware,
Southern Sung Dynasty, 1127-1278
Height: 20.6cm　　Depth: 18.2cm
Mouth dimensions: 8.2 x 6.4cm
Base dimensions: 8.9 x 7.5cm

18. 南宋　郊壇下官窯月白貫耳穿帶八方壺
　　高28公分　　口徑8.0×9.5公分
　　深21.9公分　　足徑8.6×11.1公分
　　呂一九二三
Octagonal vase with tubular handles
Chiao-t'an-hsia Kuan ware,
Southern Sung Dynasty, 1127-1278
Height: 28.0cm　　　Depth: 21.9cm
Mouth dimensions: 9.5 x 8.0cm
Base dimensions: 11.1 x 8.6cm

19. 南宋　脩內司官窯淺青投壺
　　高9.7公分　口徑2.7公分　深8.7公分　足徑3.9公分
　　呂一七九〇 71
　　Vase with two tubular handles
　　Hsiu-nei-ssu Kuan ware, Southern Sung Dynasty, 1127-1278
　　Height: 9.7cm　　　　Depth: 8.7cm
　　Mouth dimensions: 2.7cm　　　　Base dimensions: 3.9cm

20. 南宋　脩內司官窯月白投壺
　　高12.2公分　口徑2.2公分　深11.3公分　足徑4.8公分
　　呂一七九〇 102之1
　　Vase with two tubular handles
　　Hsiu-nei-ssu Kuan ware, Southern Sung Dynasty, 1127-1278
　　Height: 12.2cm　　　Depth: 11.3cm
　　Diameter: mouth 2.2cm, base 4.8cm

21. 南宋　脩內司官窯粉青弦紋瓶
　　高30.1公分　口徑9.5公分
　　深28.8公分　足徑12.7公分
　　闘四三〇 16
Vase with hopped decoration
Hsiu-nei-ssu Kuan ware,
Southern Sung Dynasty, 1127-1278
Height: 30.1cm　　Depth: 28.5cm
Diameter: mouth 9.4cm, base 4.8cm

22. 南宋　脩內司官窯粉青弦紋瓶
　　高21.7公分　口徑6.3公分　深19.9公分　足徑10.1公分
　　天五〇 46
Vase with hopped decoration
Hsiu-nei-ssu Kuan ware,
Southern Sung Dynasty, 1127-1278
Height: 21.7cm　　Depth: 19.9cm
Diameter: mouth 6.5cm, base 10.1cm

23. 南宋　脩內司官窰天青窰變弦紋瓶
　　高15.0公分　口徑4.2公分　深14.0公分　足徑5.7公分
　　呂一八〇四 37
　　Vase with hopped decoration
　　Hsiu-nei-ssu Kuan ware, Southern Sung Dynasty, 1127-1278
　　Height:　15.0cm　　　Depth:　14.0cm
　　Diameter:　mouth 4.2cm, base 5.7cm

65

24. 南宋　脩內司官窯粉青紙搥小瓶
　　高11.8公分　口徑5.4公分　深10.6公分　足徑5.9公分
　　呂一八四七 42
　　Small vase in the shape of a paper-mallet
　　Hsiu-nei-ssu Kuan ware, Southern Sung Dynasty, 1127-1278
　　Height: 11.8cm　　Depth: 10.6cm
　　Diameter: mouth 5.4cm, base 5.9cm

25. 南宋　郊壇下官窯粉青弦紋瓶
　　高22.7公分　盤口徑7.8公分
　　深22.8公分　足徑11.5公分
　　JW 1468
　　Vase with hooped decoration
　　Chiao-t'an-hsia Kuan ware,
　　Southern Sung Dynasty, 1127-1278
　　Height: 22.7cm　　Depth: 22.8cm
　　Diameter: mouth 7.8cm, base 11.5cm

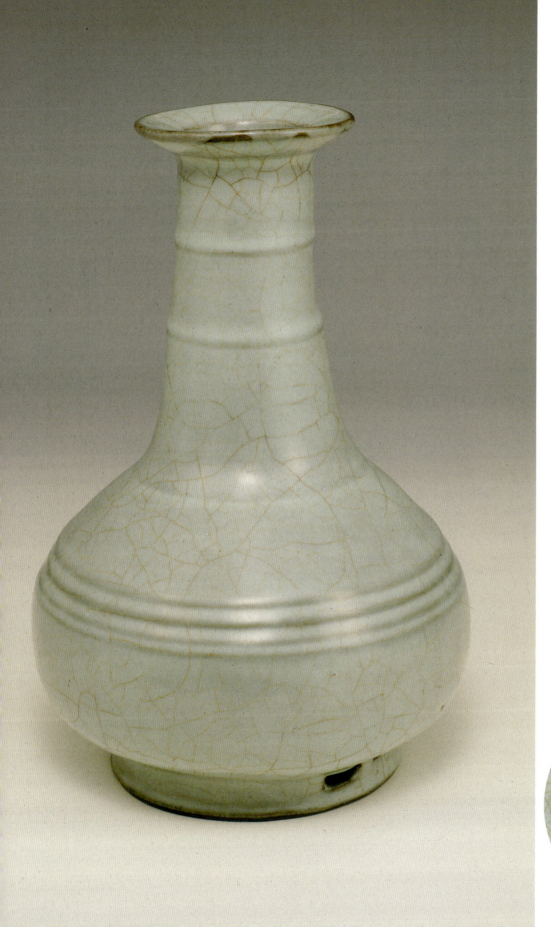

26. 南宋　郊壇下官窯灰青穿帶弦紋瓶
　　高23.6公分　口徑7.6公分
　　深21.8公分　足徑11.0公分
　　霜一八三
Vase with dish-like mouth
and hooped decoration
Chiao-t'an-hsia Kuan ware,
Southern Sung Dynasty, 1127-1278
Height: 23.6cm　　Depth: 21.8cm
Diameter: mouth 7.6cm, base 11.0cm

27. 粉青弦紋瓶（年代待考）
　　高28.6公分　　口徑6.6公分
　　深27.3公分　　底徑11.2公分
　　T 2335
　　Date unknown vase with hooped decoration
　　(date unknown)
　　Height: 28.6cm　　　Depth: 27.3cm
　　Diameter: mouth 6.6cm, base 11.2cm

28. 南宋　郊壇下官窯月白撇口瓶
　　高14.0公分　口徑4.6公分　深12.7公分　足徑5.9公分
　　呂一八〇四 21
Vase with flared mouth
Chiao-t'an-hsia Kuan ware,
Southern Sung Dynasty, 1127-1278
Height: 14.0cm　　Depth: 12.7cm
Diameter: mouth 4.6cm, base 5.9cm

29. 南宋　郊壇下官窯粉青穿帶瓶

　　高12.4公分　口徑4.4公分　深10.8公分　足徑5.2公分

　　呂一七九〇 32

Globular vase

Chiao-t'an-hsia Kuan ware,

Southern Sung Dynasty, 1127-1278

Height: 12.4cm　　　Depth: 10.8cm

Diameter: mouth 4.4cm, base 5.2cm

30. 南宋　脩內司官窯月白弦紋瓶
　　高11.8公分　口徑5.5公分　深10.6公分　足徑5.9公分
　　呂一八〇四 42
　　Vase with hopped decoration
　　Hsiu-nei-ssu Kuan ware,
　　Southern Sung Dynasty, 1127-1278
　　Height: 11.8cm　　Depth: 10.6cm
　　Diameter: mouth 5.5cm, base 5.9cm

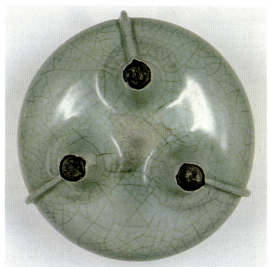

31. 北宋　官窯粉青鬲式爐
　　高12.9公分　口徑15.8公分　深7.0公分
　　呂六四一 27
Incense burner in the shape of a bronze *li*
Kuan ware, Northern Sung Dynasty, 960-1126
Height: 12.9cm　　　Depth: 7.0cm
Diameter: 15.8cm

32. 北宋　官窯月白雙耳三足爐
　　通耳高16公分　口徑30.6公分　深12.5公分
　　金一九二四
Tripodal incense burner with two handles
Kuan ware, Northern Sung Dynasty, 960-1126
Overall height: 16.0cm
Depth: 12.5cm
Mouth diameter: 30.6cm

33. 北宋　官窯月白雙耳三足爐
　　高6.6公分　深3.7公分　口徑9.9公分
　　崑二〇三 51

Tripodal incense burner with two handles
Kuan ware, Northern Sung Dynasty, 960-1126
Height: 6.6cm　　　Depth: 3.7cm
Mouth diameter: 9.6cm

34. 北宋　官窯天藍三足圓爐
　　高9.1公分　口徑10.3公分　深6.9公分　底徑9.0公分
　　呂一八〇四 80
Round tripodal incense burner
Kuan ware, Northern Sung Dynasty, 960-1126
Height: 9.1cm　　Depth: 6.9cm
Diameter: mouth 10.3cm, base 9.0cm

35. 南宋　脩內司官窯粉青簋式爐
　　高12.7公分　口徑17.5×19.7公分　深10.9公分
　　足徑15.8公分　鹹二○七 4
　　Incense burner in the shape of a bronze *kuei*
　　with hooped decorations
　　Hsiu-nei-ssu Kuan ware,
　　Southern Sung Dynasty, 1127-1278
　　Height: 12.7cm　　Depth: 10.9cm
　　Mouth dimensions: 19.7 x 17.5cm
　　Base diameter: 15.8cm

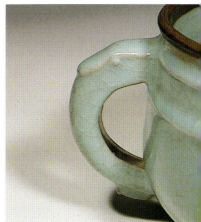

36. 南宋　郊壇下官窯灰青簋式小爐
　　高5.2公分　口徑7.2公分　足徑5.0公分
　　呂一七九〇 65
　　Small incense burner in the shape of a bronze *kuei*
　　Chiao-t'an-hsia Kuan ware,
　　Southern Sung Dynasty, 1127-1278
　　Height:　5.2cm
　　Diameter:　mouth 7.2cm, base 5.0cm

37. 宋　哥窯米邑三足圓爐
　　高8.4公分　口徑13.2公分
　　深6.4公分　底徑12.2公分　崑二二八 74
　　Round tripodal incense burner
　　Ko ware, Sung Dynasty, 960-1280
　　Height:　8.4cm　　　Depth:　6.4cm
　　Diameter:　mouth 13.2cm, base 12.2cm

38. 清　仿官釉青瓷圓爐
　　高6.6公分　口徑10.4公分　深5.0公分　足徑7.4公分
　　闕四二九 72
　　Imitation of Kuan glazed incense burner
　　Ch'ing Dynasty, 1644-1911
　　Height:　6.6cm　　　Depth:　5.0cm
　　Diameter:　mouth 10.4cm, base 14.7cm

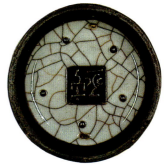

39. 南宋　脩內司官窯粉青鉢（匏）
　　高9.4公分　深8.5公分　口徑14.7公分
　　T 2014
　　Almsbowl
　　Hsiu-nei-ssu Kuan ware, Southern Sung Dynasty, 1127-1278
　　Height: 9.4cm　　　Depth: 8.5cm　　　Mouth diameter: 14.7cm

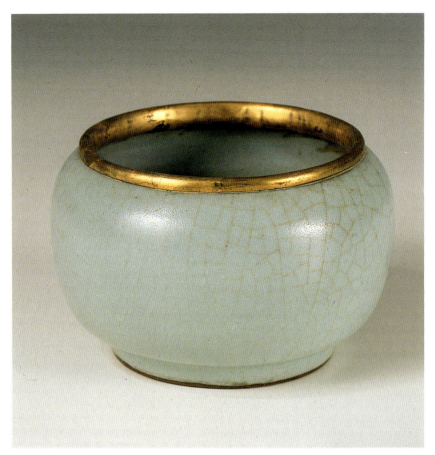

40. 南宋　脩內司官窯粉青鉢
　　高7.8公分　口徑9.8公分　足徑7.7公分
　　T 3803公分
　　Almsbowl
　　Hsiu-nei-ssu Kuan ware,
　　Southern Sung Dynasty, 1127-1278
　　Height: 7.8cm
　　Diameter: mouth 9.8cm, base 7.7cm

41. 南宋　脩內司官窯灰青鉢
　　高8.7公分　口徑13.1公分　足徑8.5公分
　　JW94
　　Almsbowl
　　Hsiu-nei-ssu Kuan ware,
　　Southern Sung Dynasty, 1127-1278
　　Height: 8.7cm
　　Diameter: mouth 13.1cm, base 8.5cm

42. 南宋　郊壇下官窯渣斗
　　高9.3公分　口徑11.9公分　深8.6公分　足徑8.4公分
　　JW96
　　Spittoon
　　Chiao-t'an-hsia Kuan ware
　　Southern Sung Dynasty, 1127-1278
　　Height: 9.3cm　　　Depth: 8.6cm
　　Diameter: mouth 11.9cm, base 8.4cm

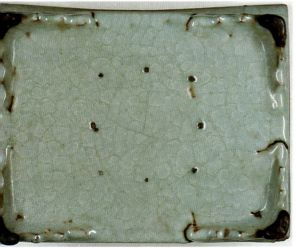

44. 南宋　脩內司官窯粉青長方盆
　　高12.5公分　口徑20.6×28.2公分　底徑19.0×24.9公分
　　雨五六八
Rectangular pot
Hsiu-nei-ssu Kuan ware, Southern Sung Dynasty, 1127-1278
Height: 12.5cm　　　Mouth dimensions: 28.2 x 20.6cm
Base dimensions: 24.9 x 19.0cm

43. 北宋　官窯天青橢圓水仙盆
　　高7.0公分　口徑23.3×16.8公分　底徑13×19.7公分
　　呂一八四六 62之1
　　Oval narcissus pot
　　Kuan ware, Northern Sung Dynasty, 960-1126
　　Height: 7.0cm　　Mouth dimensions: 23.3 x 16.8cm
　　Base dimensions: 24.9 x 19.0cm

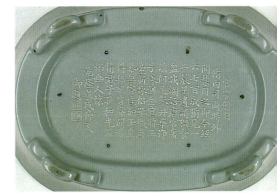

45. 北宋　官窯粉青膽瓶
高13.8公分　口徑2.4公分　深12.5公分　足徑4.7公分
呂一八〇四 34
Vase in the shape of a gall-bladder
Kuan ware, Northern Sung Dynasty, 960-1126
Height: 13.8cm　　Depth: 12.5cm
Diameter: mouth 2.4cm, base 4.7cm

46. 北宋　官窯粉青弦紋瓶
　　高13.9公分　口徑2.3公分　深12.5公分　足徑4.6公分
　　金二○四三
　　Vase with hooped decoration
　　Kuan ware, Northern Sung Dynasty, 960-1126
　　Height: 13.9cm　　Depth: 12.5cm
　　Diameter: mouth 2.3cm, base 4.6cm

47. 北宋　官窯粉青弦紋瓶
　　高18.5公分　口徑5.5公分　深17.4公分　足徑6.2公分
　　JW1474
　　Vase with hooped decoration
　　Kuan ware, Northern Sung Dynasty, 960-1126
　　Height: 18.5cm　　Depth: 17.4cm
　　Diameter: mouth 5.5cm, base 6.2cm

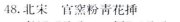

48. 北宋　官窯粉青花挿
高15.5公分　口徑7.3公分　深14.5公分　底徑4.5公分
珍二四九7
Flower receptacle
Kuan ware, Northern Sung Dynasty, 960-1126
Height: 15.5cm　　Depth: 14.5cm
Diameter: mouth 7.3cm, base 4.5cm

49. 北宋　官窯粉青花挿
高15.8公分　口徑7.5公分　深14.3公分　底徑4.5公分
呂一八四七72
Flower receptacle
Kuan ware, Northern Sung Dynasty, 960-1126
Height: 15.8cm　　Depth: 14.3cm
Diameter: mouth 7.5cm, base 4.5cm

50. 南宋　脩內司官窰粉青花揷
　　高17.2公分　口徑9.0公分　深16.4公分　底徑6.9公分
　　呂一七九〇 54
　　Flower receptacle
　　Hsiu-nei-ssu Kuan ware, Southern Sung Dynasty, 1127-1278
　　Height: 17.2cm　　Depth: 16.4cm
　　Diameter: mouth 9.0cm, base 6.9cm

51. 南宋　脩內司官窯淺粉青花挿
　　高14.7公分　口徑7.6公分　深12.7公分　底徑5.1公分
　　金一九八三
Flower receptacle
Hsiu-nei-ssu Kuan ware,
Southern Sung Dynasty, 1127-1278
Height: 14.7cm　　Depth: 12.7cm
Diameter: mouth 7.6cm, base 5.1cm

52. 南宋　郊壇下官窯灰青海棠式花挿
　　高22.6公分　口徑16.5×12.5公分
　　深21.3公分　足徑8.2×5.9公分
　　出二二七 19
Flower receptacle with begonia-shaped rim
Chiao-t'an-hsia Kuan ware,
Southern Sung Dynasty, 1127-1278
Height: 22.6cm　　Depth: 21.3cm
Mouth dimensions: 16.5 x 12.5cm
Base dimensions: 8.2 x 5.9cm

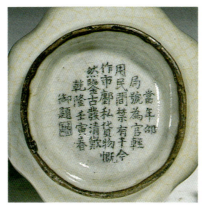

53. 南宋　脩內司官窯月白凹稜膽瓶
　　高16.0公分　口徑3.0公分　深13.9公分　足徑5.7公分
　　呂一八〇四10
Gall-bladder shaped vase with fluted corners
Hsiu-nei-ssu Kuan ware,
Southern Sung Dynasty, 1127-1278
Height: 16.0cm　　Depth: 13.9cm
Diameter: mouth 3.0cm, base 5.7cm

54. 南宋　郊壇下官窯月白海棠式貫耳瓶
　　高16.6公分　口徑4.6×5.4公分　深15.3公分
　　足徑4.8×5.9公分　呂一八〇四5
　　Vase with tubular handles and begonia-shaped rim
　　Chiao-t'an-hsia Kuan ware, Southern Sung Dynasty, 1127-1278
　　Height: 16.4cm　　　Depth: 15.3cm
　　Mouth dimensions: 5.4 x 4.6cm
　　Base dimensions: 5.9 x 4.8cm

55. 南宋　郊壇下官窯粉青海棠式小瓶
　　高11.3公分　口徑3.3×5.5公分　深9.7公分
　　足徑3.3×4.4公分　呂一八〇四8
　　Small vase with begonia-shaped rim
　　Chiao-t'an-hsia Kuan ware, Southern Sung Dynasty, 1127-1278
　　Height: 11.3cm　　　Depth: 9.7cm
　　Mouth dimensions: 5.5 x 3.3cm
　　Base dimensions: 4.4 x 3.3cm

56. 南宋　郊壇下官窯灰青葫蘆瓶
高18.7公分　口徑1.9公分
深18.3公分　足徑5.7公分　JW130
Gourd-shaped vase
Chiao-t'an-hsia Kuan ware,
Southern Sung Dynasty, 1127-1278
Height: 18.7cm.　Depth: 18.3cm
Diameter: mouth 1.9cm, base 5.7cm

57. 南宋　脩內司官窯月白葫蘆瓶
高23.7公分　口徑3.1公分　深22.7公分　足徑8.4公分
金二八一[37]
Gourd-shaped vase
Hsiu-nei-ssu Kuan ware, Southern Sung Dynasty, 1127-1278
Height: 23.7cm　　Depth: 22.7cm
Diameter: mouth 3.1cm, base 8.4cm

58. 南宋　脩內司官窯粉青葵花式洗
　　高9.3公分　面徑16.0×16.9公分
　　雨四八五
　　Hibiscus-shaped brush washer
　　Hsiu-nei-ssu Kuan ware,
　　Southern Sung Dynasty, 1127-1278
　　Height: 9.3cm
　　Mouth dimensions: 16.9 x 16.0cm

59. 南宋　脩內司官窯月白雙蓮房水注
　　高7.2公分　蓮蓬面徑7.3公分　盛口徑8.0公分
　　崑二二七6
　　Double lotus-pod shaped water dropper
　　Hsiu-nei-ssu Kuan ware,
　　Southern Sung Dynasty, 1127-1278
　　Height: 7.2cm
　　Diameter: lotus petals 7.3cm, vessel mouth 8.0cm

60. 北宋　官窯天青臂擱
　　高2.0公分　長22.5公分　寬5.9公分
　　呂一七九〇 25
　　Armrest
　　Kuan ware, Northern Sung Dynasty, 960-1126
　　Height: 2.0cm　　　Length: 22.5cm

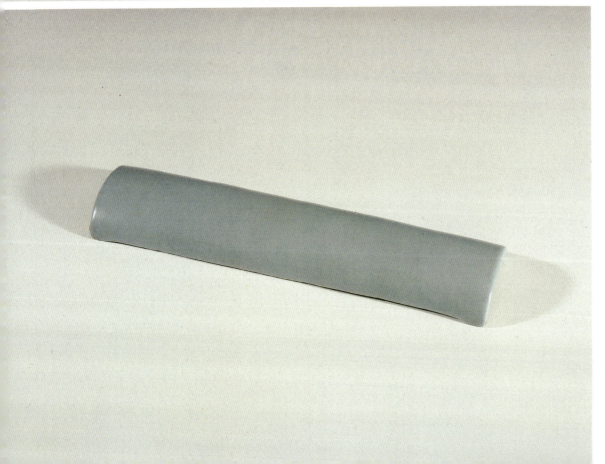

61. 北宋　官窯月白小水注
　　高3.2公分　面徑4.3公分　底徑4.3公分
　　呂一七九○56之2
　　Small water dropper
　　Kuan ware, Northern Sung Dynasty, 960-1126
　　Height: 3.2cm　　　Diameter: 4.3cm

62. 北宋　官窯粉青筆筒
　　高9.8公分　深8.6公分　口徑7.7公分　足徑7.3公分
　　呂一七九○82
　　Brush holder
　　Kuan ware, Northern Sung Dynasty, 960-1126
　　Height: 9.8cm
　　Diameter: mouth 7.7cm, base 7.3cm

99

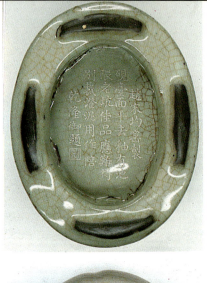

63. 南宋　脩內司官窯淺青橢圓硯
　　高5.2公分　口徑10.4×13.7公分　足徑10.4×13.7公分
　　天一一三七
　　Oval inkstone
　　Hsiu-nei-ssu Kuan ware,
　　Southern Sung Dynasty, 1127-1278
　　Height : 5.2cm
　　Mouth dimensions: 13.7 x 10.4cm
　　Base dimensions: 13.7 x 10.4cm


64. 南宋　脩內司官窯月白葵花式水盛
　　高4.5公分　口徑7.0公分分　深3.4公分
　　爲四九一 5
　　Floral-shaped water container
　　Hsiu-nei-ssu Kuan ware,
　　Southern Sung Dynasty, 1127-1278
　　Height : 4.5cm
　　Diameter: mouth 7.0cm, base: 3.4cm

65. 清　仿官釉筆架

　高5.0公分　長13公分　底長13公分　底寬3.4公分

　闕五〇一25

Brush stand with imitation Kuan glaze
Ch'ing Dynasty, 1644-1911
Height: 5.0cm　　　Length: 13.0cm
Base: maximum length 13.0cm, maximum width 3.4cm

66. 南宋　郊壇下官窯天青葉式洗
　　高4.5～5.7公分　面長23.5公分
　　藏一二六<sup>47</sup>
Leaf-shaped brush washer
Chiao-t'an-hsia Kuan ware,
Southern Sung Dynasty, 1127-1278
Height: 4.5-5.7cm　　Length: 23.5cm

67. 北宋　官窯粉青葵花式小盌
　　高4.8公分　口徑11.4×11.8公分　足徑3.7公分
　　呂一七九○ 12之2
Small floral-shaped bowl
Kuan ware, Northern Sung Dynasty, 960-1126
Height: 4.8cm
Mouth dimensions: 11.8 x 11.4cm
Base diameter: 3.7cm

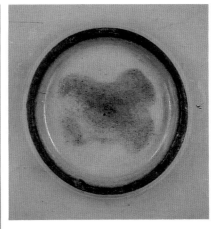

68. 北宋　官窯粉青葵花式小盌
　　高4.9公分　口徑11.5×12.1公分　足徑3.7公分
　　呂一七九○ 12之1
Small floral-shaped bowl
Kuan ware, Northern Sung Dynasty, 960-1126
Height: 4.9cm
Mouth dimensions: 12.1 x 11.4cm
Base diameter: 3.7cm

69.清　乾隆仿官釉葵花口盌
　　高5.5公分　　口徑11.9×12.2公分　　足徑4.3公分
　　歲四七〇 1
　　Bowl with foliated rim
　　Ch'ien-lung period, 1736-1795 imitation of Kuan ware
　　Height: 5.5cm
　　Mouth dimensions: 12.5 x 11.9cm
　　Base diameter: 4.3cm

70. 北宋　官窯粉青梅花式楛
　　高2.5公分　口徑6.5公分　足徑10.1公分
　　天一一三三
　　Plum blossom-shaped cup
　　Kuan ware, Northern Sung Dynasty, 960-1126
　　Height: 2.5cm
　　Diameter: mouth 6.5cm, Base 10.1cm

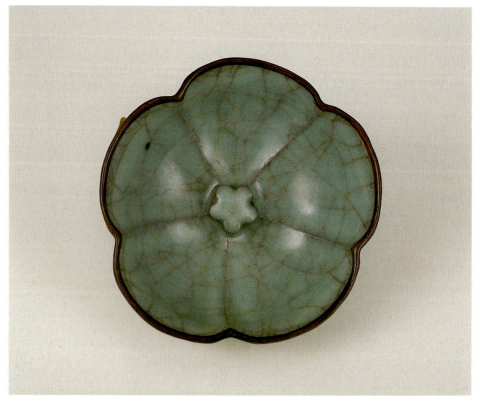

71. 北宋　官窯天青菱花式小盌
　　高5.5公分　口徑8.5×9.5公分　足徑3.1公分
　　呂一七九○ 96
　　Small floral-shaped bowl
　　Kuan ware, Northern Sung Dynasty, 960-1126
　　Height：5.5cm
　　Mouth dimensions：9.5 x 8.5cm
　　Base diameter：3.1cm

72. 北宋　官窯粉青蓮花式花插
　　通高5.5公分　盌高5.0公分
　　口徑11.3公分　足徑4.7公分
　　呂一七九〇 76

Lotus-shaped flower receptacle
Kuan ware, Northern Sung Dynasty, 960-1126
Height: lotus 5.5cm, vessel rim 5.0cm
Diameter: mouth 11.3cm, base 4.7cm

73. 南宋　郊壇下官窯灰青牡丹花式栥
　　高3.8公分　口徑7.3×7.9公分　足徑3.1公分
　　金七八 1之2
　　Cup with peony-shaped rim
　　Chiao-t'an-hsia Kuan ware,
　　Southern Sung Dynasty, 1127-1278
　　Height: 3.8cm　　　Mouth dimensions: 7.9 x 7.3cm
　　Base diameter: 3.1cm

74. 南宋　脩內司官窯粉青八方桮
　　高4.3公分　口徑8.3×8.5公分　深3.6公分
　　足徑3.5×3.2公分　呂一七九〇 51
Octagonal cup
Hsiu-nei-ssu Kuan ware, Southern Sung Dynasty, 1127-1278
Height: 4.3cm　　　　Depth: 3.6cm
Mouth dimensions: 8.5 x 8.3cm
Base dimensions: 3.5 x 3.2cm

75. 南宋　脩內司官窯粉青把桮
　　高3.9公分　深3.1公分　口徑7.9公分　足徑3.4公分
　　金七八 11
Cup with handle
Hsiu-nei-ssu Kuan ware,
Southern Sung Dynasty, 1127-1278
Height: 3.9cm　　　　Depth: 31.cm
Diameter: mouth 7.9cm, base 3.4cm

76.北宋　官窯月白八方盤
　　高3.4公分　口徑18.1×18.8公分
　　足徑5.7×6.2公分闕四二九 55
　　Octagonal dish
　　Kuan ware, Northern Sung Dynasty, 960-1126
　　Height:　3.4cm
　　Mouth dimensions:　18.8x 18.1 cm
　　Base dimensions:　6.2 x 5.7cm

77. 南宋　脩內司官窯月白葵口碟
　　高2.5公分　口徑15.0×15.5公分　足徑5.5公分
　　闕四三〇 76

Dish with hibiscus petal rim
Hsiu-nei-ssu Kuan ware,
Southern Sung Dynasty, 1127-1278
Height: 2.5cm
Mouth dimensions: 15.5 x 15.0cm
Base diameter: 5.5cm

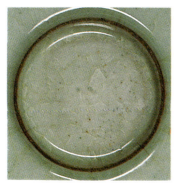

78. 南宋　脩內司官窯灰青劃花蟠龍碟
　　高1.8公分　口徑13.0公分　足徑3.8公分
　　闕四三〇 102

Dish with incised coiled dragon design
Hsiu-nei-ssu Kuan ware,
Southern Sung Dynasty, 1127-1278
Height: 1.8cm
Diameter: mouth 13.0cm, base 3.8cm

79. 南宋　郊壇下官窯灰青葵口碟
　　高2.9公分　口徑15.4公分　底徑6.1公分
　　JW150
　　Dish with foliated petal rim
　　Chiao-t'an-hsia Kuan ware,
　　Southern Sung Dynasty, 1127-1278
　　Height: 2.9cm
　　Diameter: mouth 15.4cm, base 6.1cm

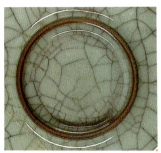

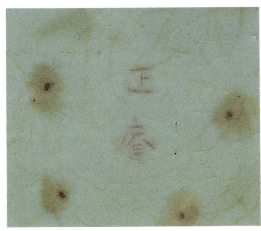

80. 南宋　脩內司官窯粉青圓洗
　　高5.2公分　口徑15.5公分　底徑13.5公分
　　闕四三〇 112
　　Round basin
　　Hsiu-nei-ssu Kuan ware,
　　Southern Sung Dynasty, 1127-1278
　　Height: 5.2cm
　　Diameter: mouth 15.5cm, base 13.5cm

81. 南宋　郊壇下官窯圓洗
　　高5.2公分　口徑12.4公分　底徑11.5公分
　　JW129
　　Round basin
　　Chiao-t'an-hsia Kuan ware,
　　Southern Sung Dynasty, 1127-1278
　　Height: 5.2cm
　　Diameter: mouth 12.4cm, base 11.5cm

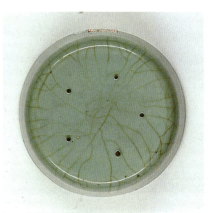

82. 南宋　脩內司官窯粉青彫龍圓洗
　　高4.7公分　口徑18.4公分
　　底徑16.5公分　墊燒底徑1.2公分
　　金二四七 51之1
　　Round basin with dragon design in relief
　　Hsiu-nei-ssu Kuan ware, Southern Sung Dynasty, 1127-1278
　　Height: 4.7cm
　　Diameter: mouth 18.4cm, base 16.5cm, stand 12.0cm

83. 南宋　脩內司官窯粉青大圓洗
　　高6.5公分　口徑26.4公分　底徑23.5公分
　　呂一九三二

Round large basin
Hsiu-nei-ssu Kuan ware,
Southern Sung Dynasty, 1127-1278
Height: 6.5cm
Diameter: mouth 26.4cm, base 23.5cm

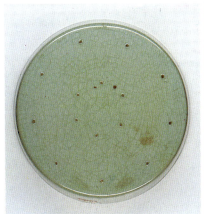

84. 南宋　郊壇下官窯灰青葵瓣口小洗
　　高4.4公分　口徑11.0公分　足徑7.5公分
　　麗一一九三 3
Small basin with foliated rim
Chiao-t'an-hsia Kuan ware,
Southern Sung Dynasty, 1127,1278
Height: 4.4cm
Diameter: mouth 11.0cm, base 7.5cm

85. 南宋　脩內司官窯粉青蔗段圓洗
高6.0公分　口徑19.0公分　底徑15.9公分
闕四二九 49
Round basin with cut sugarcane design
Hsiu-nei-ssu Kuan ware,
Southern Sung Dynasty, 1127-1278
Height: 6.0cm
Diameter: mouth 19.0cm, base 15.9cm

86. 南宋　脩內司官窯淺青葵瓣口洗
　　高3.8公分　口徑12.0公分　足徑8.2公分
　　呂一八四六 19

Basin with foliated rim
Hsiu-nei-ssu Kuan ware,
Southern Sung Dynasty, 1127-1278
Height: 3.8cm
Diameter: mouth 12.0cm, base 8.2cm

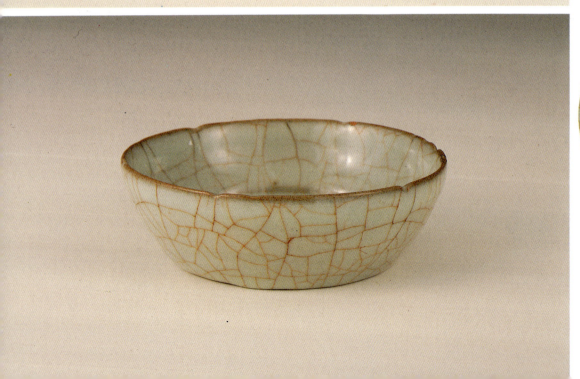

87. 南宋　脩內司官窰粉青葵瓣口洗
　　高4.3公分　口徑12.0公分　足徑7.8公分
　　崑一六一 3

Basin with foliated rim
Hsiu-nei-ssu Kuan ware,
Southern Sung Dynasty, 1127-1278
Height: 4.3cm
Diameter: mouth 12.0cm, base 7.8cm

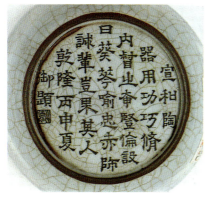

124

88. 南宋　脩內司官窯粉青大圓盤
　　高5.5公分　口徑23.5公分　足徑7.7公分
　　金二八〇 70之3
　　Large round dish
　　Hsiu-nei-ssu Kuan ware,
　　Southern Sung Dynasty, 1127-1278
　　Diameter: mouth 23.0cm, base 7.7cm
　　Height: 5.5cm

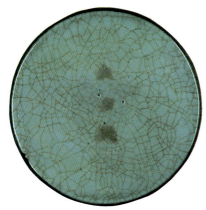

89. 南宋　郊壇下官窯灰青大圓盤
　　高6.5公分　口徑27.0公分　足徑10.2公分
　　JW163
　　Large round dish
　　Chiao-t'an-hsia Kuan ware,
　　Southern Sung Dynasty, 1127-1278
　　Height: 6.5cm
　　Diameter: mouth 27.0cm, base 10.2cm

90. 南宋　脩內司官窯粉青大圓盤
　　高4.4公分　口徑19.2公分　足徑11.7公分
　　闕五○一11
Round dish
Hsiu-nei-ssu Kuan ware,
Southern Sung Dynasty, 1127-1278
Height: 4.4cm
Diameter: mouth 19.2cm, base 11.7cm

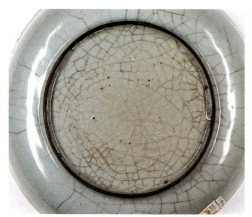

91. 南宋　郊壇下官窯粉青葵瓣口龍紋盤
　　高4.4公分　口徑19.2公分　足徑11.7公分
　　T 2487
Dish with foliated rim and dragon decor Chiao-t'an-hsia Kuan ware

92. 南宋　脩內司官窯粉青菱花式盤
　　高5.3公分　口徑18.2×17.5公分　足徑11.5公分
　　崑二二八 41
　　Lobed dish with foliated rim
　　Hsiu-nei-ssu Kuan ware,
　　Southern Sung Dynasty, 1127-1278
　　Height: 5.3cm
　　Mouth dimensions: 18.2 x 17.5cm
　　Base diameter: 11.5cm

93. 南宋　脩內司官窯粉青蓮花式盤
　　高4.6公分　口徑18.0公分　足徑11.5公分
　　金二〇五六
　　Lobed dish foliated rim
　　Hsiu-nei-ssu Kuan ware,
　　Southern Sung Dynasty, 1127-1278
　　Height:　4.6cm
　　Diameter:　mouth 18.0cm, base 11.5cm

94. 南宋　脩內司官窯粉青牡丹花式盤
　　高3.5公分　口徑12.8×13.4公分　足徑9.2公分
　　麗一〇五八 14之2
Lobed dish with foliated rim
Hsiu-nei-ssu Kuan ware,
Southern Sung Dynasty, 1127-1278
Height: 3.5cm
Mouth dimensions: 13.4 x 12.8cm
Base diameter: 9.2cm

95. 南宋　郊壇下官窯粉青菊花式盤
　　高4.5公分　口徑18.5公分　足徑13.3公分
　　JW162

Chrysanthemum-shaped dish
Chiao-t'an-hsia Kuan ware,
Southern Sung Dynasty, 1127-1278
Height: 4.5cm
Diameter: mouth 18.5cm, base 13.3cm

96. 南宋　脩內司官窯粉青蓮瓣盤
　　高3.9公分　口徑16.9公分　足徑12.0公分
　　闕四三〇 20之7
Lobed dish with foliated rim
Hsiu-nei-ssu Kuan ware,
Southern Sung Dynasty, 1127-1278
Height: 3.9cm
Diameter: mouth 16.9cm, base 12.0cm

97. 南宋　脩內司官窯天青蓮瓣盤
　　高4.4公分　口徑15.3公分　足徑9.2公分
　　奈三九六 25

Dish with lotus petal shaped lobes
Hsiu-nei-ssu Kuan ware,
Southern Sung Dynasty, 1127-1278
Height: 4.4cm
Diameter: mouth 15.3cm, base 9.2cm

98. 南宋　脩內司官窯粉青葵花式盤
　　高5.3公分　口徑22.0公分　足徑6.0公分
　　麗一一二九 3之15
Dish with foliated rim
Hsiu-nei-ssu Kuan ware,
Southern Sung Dynasty, 1127-1278
Height: 5.3cm
Diameter: mouth 22.0cm, base 6.0cm

99. 南宋　脩內司官窯翠青葵花式盤
　　高4.5公分　口徑18.0公分　足徑5.6公分
　　巨一八一<sup>29</sup>
Dish with foliated rim
Hsiu-nei-ssu Kuan ware,
Southern Sung Dynasty, 1127-1278
Height: 4.5cm
Diameter: mouth 18.0cm, base 5.6cm

100. 南宋　脩內司官窯粉青葵花式盤
　　高4.6公分　口徑19.0公分　足徑6.0公分
　　麗一〇五八 14之1
Dish with foliated rim
Hsiu-nei-ssu Kuan ware,
Southern Sung Dynasty, 1127-1278
Height: 4.6cm
Diameter: mouth 19.0cm, base 6.0cm

101. 南宋 脩內司官窯粉青葵花式盤
高5.5公分　口徑23.5公分　足徑7.7公分
金二八〇 70之2
Dish with foliated rim
Hsiu-nei-ssu Kuan ware,
Southern Sung Dynasty, 1127-1278
Height: 5.5cm
Diameter: mouth 23.5cm, base 7.7cm

102. 南宋　脩內司官窯粉青葵花式盤
　　　高4.6公分　口徑19.2公分　足徑6.5公分
　　　闕五○─12
　　　Dish with foliated rim
　　　Hsiu-nei-ssu Kuan ware,
　　　Southern Sung Dynasty, 1127-1278
　　　Height: 4.6cm
　　　Diameter: mouth 19.2cm, base 6.5cm

103. 南宋　脩內司官窯天青葵花式盌
　　　高7.2公分　口徑19.0公分　足徑6.1公分
　　　珍四五之1
　　　Dish with foliated rim
　　　Hsiu-nei-ssu Kuan ware,
　　　Southern Sung Dynasty, 1127-1278
　　　Height:  7.2cm
　　　Diameter:  mouth 19.0cm, base 6.1cm

104. 南宋　脩內司官窯粉青葵花式淺盌
　　　高5.5公分　口徑20.1公分　足徑7.1公分
　　　闕四三○ 122
　　　Shall bowl with foliated rim
　　　Hsiu-nei-ssu Kuan ware,
　　　Southern Sung Dynasty, 1127-1278
　　　Height: 5.5cm
　　　Diameter: mouth 20.1cm, base 7.1cm

105. 南宋　脩內司官窯粉青葵花式盌
　　 高5.8公分　口徑17.9公分　足徑5.7公分
　　 闕四三〇 50
Bowl with foliated rim
Hsiu-nei-ssu Kuan ware,
Southern Sung Dynasty, 1127-1278
Height: 5.8cm
Diameter: mouth 17.9cm, base 5.7cm

106. 南宋　郊壇下官窯灰青葵花式盌
　　　高6.7公分　口徑19.6公分　足徑5.9公分
　　　麗一〇五七6

Bowl with foliated rim
Chiao-t'an-hsia Kuan ware,
Southern Sung Dynasty, 1127-1278
Height: 6.7cm
Diameter: mouth 19.6cm, base 5.9cm

107. 南宋　脩內司官窯粉青葵花式大盌
　　　高8.8公分　口徑23.1公分　足徑6.1公分
　　　律一四八 30之2

Large bowl with foliated rim
Hsiu-nei-ssu Kuan ware,
Southern Sung Dynasty, 1127-1278
Height: 8.8cm
Diameter: mouth 23.1cm, base 6.1cm

108. 南宋　脩內司官窰月白大盌
　　　高9.0公分　口徑20.9公分　足徑5.9公分
　　　闞四三〇 65
　　　Large bowl
　　　Hsiu-nei-ssu Kuan ware,
　　　Southern Sung Dynasty, 1127-1278
　　　Height: 9.0cm
　　　Diameter: mouth 20.9cm, base 5.9cm

109. 南宋　脩內司官窯粉青葵口大盌
　　　高9.4公分　口徑20.8公分　足徑6.5公分
　　　JW160
　　　Large bowl with foliated rim
　　　Hsiu-nei-ssu Kuan ware,
　　　Southern Sung Dynasty, 1127-1278
　　　Height: 9.4cm
　　　Diameter: mouth 20.8cm, base 6.5cm

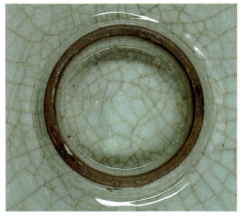

110. 南宋　脩內司官窯粉青菊瓣盌
　　　高8.5公分　口徑17.5公分　足徑4.9公分
　　　律一四八 29之2
　　　Bowl with moulded chrysanthemum
　　　petal shaped lobes
　　　Hsiu-nei-ssu Kuan ware,
　　　Southern Sung Dynasty, 1127-1278
　　　Height: 8.5cm
　　　Diameter: mouth 17.5cm, base 4.9cm

111. 宋　龍泉窯天青蓮瓣盌
　　高8.5公分　口徑17.5公分　足徑4.9公分
　　律一四七 15之1
　　Bowl with lotus petal shaped lobes
　　Lung-ch'uan ware,
　　Sung Dynasty, 960-1278
　　Height: 8.5cm
　　Diameter: mouth 17.5cm, base 4.9cm

112. 宋　龍泉窯粉青盌
　　高5.8公分　口徑16.5公分　足徑4.0公分
　　律一四八 4
　　Hat-shaped bowl
　　Hung-ch'uan ware,
　　Sung Dynasty, 960-1278
　　Height: 5.8cm
　　Diameter: mouth 16.5cm, base 4.0cm

113. 南宋　脩內司官窯粉青盌
　　 高5.6公分　口徑16.4公分　足徑4.9公分
　　 闕四三○42
　　 Small shallow bowl
　　 Hsiu-nei-ssu Kuan ware,
　　 Southern Sung Dynasty, 1127-1278
　　 Height: 5.6cm
　　 Diameter: mouth 16.4cm, base 4.9cm

114. 南宋　郊壇下官窯粉青葵瓣口盌
　　　高5.3公分　口徑14.0公分　足徑3.4公分
　　　律一四八 17之2
　　　Small shallow bowl with foliated rim
　　　Chiao-t'an-hsia Kuan ware,
　　　Southern Sung Dynasty, 1127-1278
　　　Height: 5.3cm
　　　Diameter: mouth 14.0cm, base 3.4cm

115. 南宋　脩內司官窯粉青盌
　　 高4.6公分　口徑10.4公分　足徑2.5公分
　　 呂一七九○ 40之2
　　 Small shallow bowl
　　 Hsiu-nei-ssu Kuan ware,
　　 Southern Sung Dynasty, 1127-1278
　　 Height: 4.6cm
　　 Diameter: mouth 10.4cm, base 2.5cm

116. 南宋　郊壇下官窯粉青葵瓣口盌
　　　高5.1公分　口徑13.7公分　足徑3.6公分
　　　珍二四九 3
　　　Small shallow bowl with foliated rim
　　　Chiao-t'an-hsia Kuan ware,
　　　Southern Sung Dynasty, 1127-1278

117. 宋　龍泉窯翠青盌
　　　高5.2公分　口徑13.7公分　足徑3.1公分
　　　珍二四九 5
　　　Small shallow bowl
　　　Lung-ch'uan ware, Sung Dynasty, 960-1278
　　　Height: 5.2cm
　　　Diameter: mouth 13.7cm, base 3.1cm

118. 南宋　郊壇下官窯灰青葵瓣口碟
　　　高2.6公分　口徑14.4公分　足徑7.3公分
　　　麗一一二九3之8
　　　Dish with foliated rim
　　　Chiao-t'an-hsia Kuan ware,
　　　Southern Sung Dynasty, 1127-1278
　　　Height: 2.6cm
　　　Diameter: mouth 14.4cm, base 7.3cm

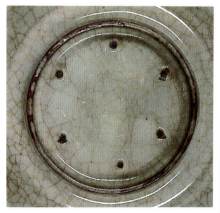

119. 南宋　郊壇下官窯灰青葵瓣口碟
　　　高2.2公分　口徑14.1公分　足徑7.5公分
　　　麗一一二九 3之9

Dish with foliated rim
Chiao-t'an-hsia Kuan ware,
Southern Sung Dynasty, 1127-1278
Height: 2.2cm
Diameter: mouth 14.1cm, base 7.5cm

120. 南宋　郊壇下官窯灰青葵瓣口碟
　　　高3.1公分　口徑14.2公分　足徑7.2公分
　　　闕四三〇 94之1
　　　Dish with foliated rim
　　　Chiao-t'an-hsia Kuan ware,
　　　Southern Sung Dynasty, 1127-1278
　　　Height: 3.1cm
　　　Diameter: mouth 14.2cm, base 7.2cm

121. 南宋　脩內司官窯淺青葵瓣口碟
　　 高3.0公分　口徑13.8公分　足徑7.2公分
　　 律一四八 14之1

Dish with foliated rim
Hsiu-nei-ssu Kuan ware,
Southern Sung Dynasty, 1127-1278
Height: 3.0cm
Diameter: mouth 13.8cm, base 7.2cm

122. 南宋　郊壇下官窯月白葵瓣口碟
　　　高4.6公分　口徑18.6公分　足徑6.0公分
　　　麗一〇七六2
Dish with foliated rim
Chiao-t'an-hsia Kuan ware,
Southern Sung Dynasty, 1127-1278
Height: 4.6cm
Diameter: mouth 18.6cm, base 6.0cm

123. 南宋　脩內司官窯月白葵瓣口碟
    高2.5公分　口徑17.0公分　足徑9.0公分
    金一九八二1
Dish with foliated rim
Hsiu-nei-ssu Kuan ware,
Southern Sung Dynasty, 1127-1278
Height: 2.5cm
Diameter: mouth 17.0cm, base 9.0cm

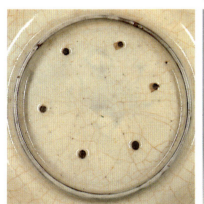

124. 南宋　脩內司官窯月白葵瓣口碟
　　　高2.9公分　口徑17.1公分　底徑9.3公分
　　　JW95
　　　Dish with foliated rim
　　　Hsiu-nei-ssu Kuan ware,
　　　Southern Sung Dynasty, 1127-1278
　　　Height: 2.9cm
　　　Diameter: mouth 17.1cm, base 9.3cm

125. 南宋　脩內司官窯月白葵瓣口碟
　　　高2.5公分　口徑14.5公分　足徑5.5公分
　　　麗一一二九 3之12

Dish with foliated rim
Hsiu-nei-ssu Kuan ware,
Southern Sung Dynasty, 1127-1278
Height: 2.5cm
Diameter: mouth 14.5cm, base 5.5cm

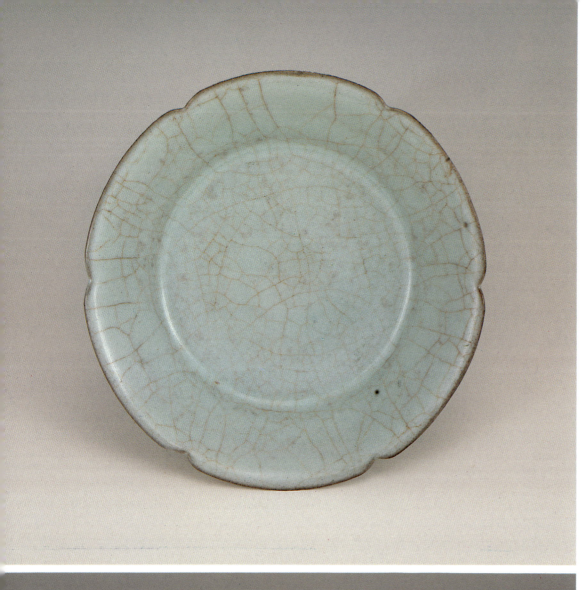

126. 南宋　脩內司官窯淺青葵瓣口碟
　　　高3.2公分　口徑13.2公分　足徑5.4公分
　　　闞五〇一-30
　　　Dish with foliated rim
　　　Hsiu-nei-ssu Kuan ware,
　　　Southern Sung Dynasty, 1127-1278
　　　Height:　3.2cm
　　　Diameter:　mouth 13.2cm, base 5.4cm

127. 南宋　脩內司官窯灰青葵瓣口碟
　　　高2.9公分　口徑14.6公分　底徑5.7公分
　　　JW97

Dish with foliated rim
Hsiu-nei-ssu Kuan ware,
Southern Sung Dynasty, 1127-1278
Height: 2.9cm
Diameter: mouth 14.6cm, base 5.7cm

128. 南宋　脩內司官窯月白葵瓣口碟
　　高3.1公分　口徑14.6公分　足徑5.8公分
　　闕四三○ 20之2
Dish with foliated rim
Hsiu-nei-ssu Kuan ware,
Southern Sung Dynasty, 1127-1278
Height: 2.9cm
Diameter: mouth 14.6cm, base 5.7cm

129. 南宋　脩內司官窯月白葵瓣口碟
　　　高3.3公分　口徑14.5公分　足徑5.6公分
　　　麗一一二九 3之11
　　　Dish with foliated rim
　　　Hsiu-nei-ssu Kuan ware,
　　　Southern Sung Dynasty, 1127-1278
　　　Height: 3.3cm
　　　Diameter: mouth 14.5cm, base 5.6cm

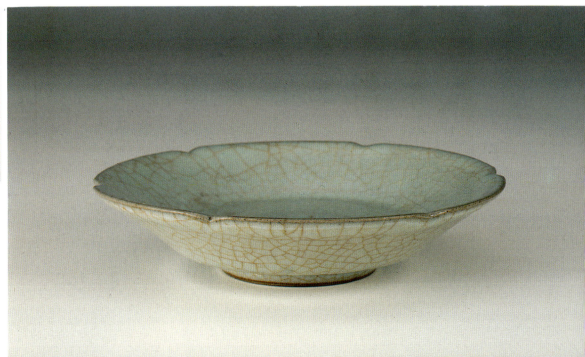

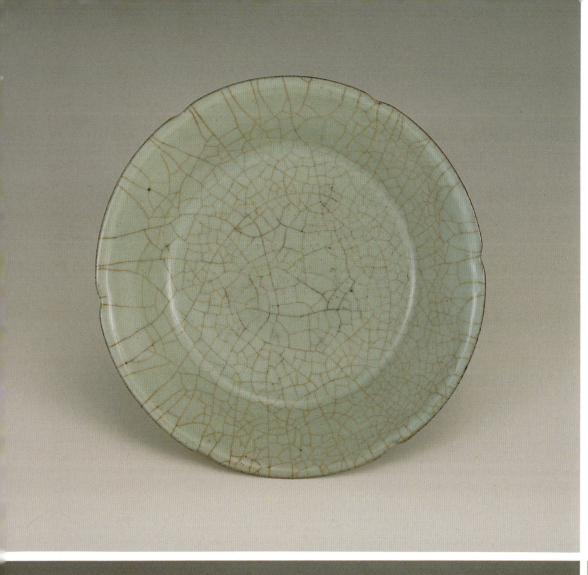

130. 南宋　脩內司官窯月白葵瓣口碟
　　 高3.2公分　口徑14.3公分　足徑5.9公分
　　 闕四三〇 82

Dish with foliated rim
Hsiu-nei-ssu Kuan ware,
Southern Sung Dynasty, 1127-1278
Height: 3.2cm
Diameter: mouth 14.3cm, base 5.9cm

131. 南宋　脩內司官窯月白葵瓣口碟
　　　高3.0公分　口徑14.4公分　足徑6.0公分
　　　闕四三〇 74
　　　Dish with foliated rim
　　　Hsiu-nei-ssu Kuan ware,
　　　Southern Sung Dynasty, 1127-1278
　　　Height: 3.0cm
　　　Diameter: mouth 14.4cm, base 6.0cm

132. 南宋　郊壇下官窯灰青菊瓣口碟
　　　高2.3公分　　口徑15.4公分　　足徑8.1公分
　　　麗一一二九 3之2

Dish with foliated rim
Chiao-t'an-hsia Kuan ware,
Southern Sung Dynasty, 1127-1278
Height: 2.3cm
Diameter: mouth 15.4cm, base 8.1cm

133. 南宋　郊壇下官窯灰青菊瓣口碟
　　 高2.7公分　口徑15.4公分　足徑8.1公分
　　 麗一一二九 3之3
　　 Dish with foliated rim
　　 Chiao-t'an-hsia Kuan ware,
　　 Southern Sung Dynasty, 1127-1278
　　 Height:　2.7cm
　　 Diameter:　mouth 15.4cm, base 8.1cm

134. 南宋　郊壇下官窯粉青葵瓣口碟
　　　高2.9公分　口徑14.5公分　足徑6.0公分
　　　闕四三〇 20之3
　　　Dish with foliated rim
　　　Chiao-t'an-hsia Kuan ware,
　　　Southern Sung Dynasty, 1127-1278
　　　Height: 2.9cm
　　　Diameter: mouth 14.5cm, base 6.0cm

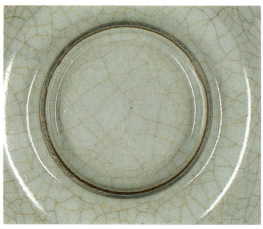

135. 南宋　脩內司官窯月白牡丹花式洗
　　　高3.5公分　口徑11.5公分　足徑8.8公分
　　　麗一一二九 3之16
　　　Floral-shaped basin
　　　Hsiu-nei-ssu Kuan ware,
　　　Southern Sung Dynasty, 1127-1278
　　　Height: 3.5cm
　　　Diameter: mouth 11.5cm, base 8.8cm

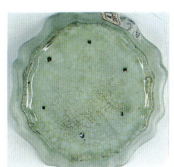

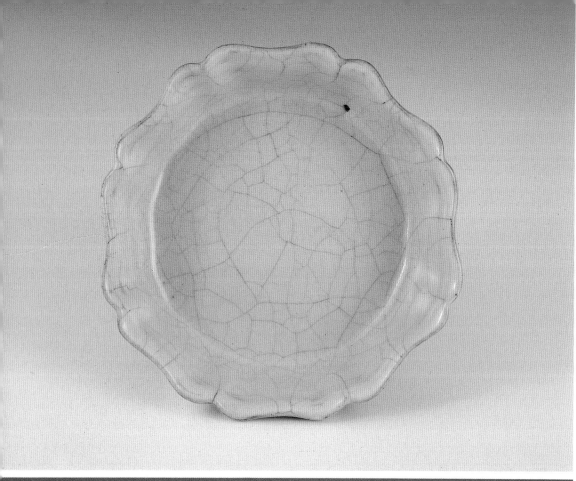

136. 南宋　脩內司官窯月白牡丹花式洗
　　 高3.5公分　口徑11.6公分　足徑9.2公分
　　 麗一六五八
　　 Floral-shaped basin
　　 Hsiu-nei-ssu Kuan ware,
　　 Southern Sung Dynasty, 1127-1278
　　 Height: 3.5cm
　　 Diameter: mouth 11.6cm, base 9.2cm

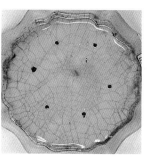

137. 南宋　脩內司官窯粉青牡丹花式洗
　　　高3.4公分　口徑12.1公分　足徑8.9公分
　　　柰四七九14
　　　Floral-shaped basin
　　　Hsiu-nei-ssu Kuan ware,
　　　Southern Sung Dynasty, 1127-1278
　　　Height: 3.4cm
　　　Diameter: mouth 12.1cm, base 8.9cm

138. 南宋　郊壇下官窰灰青牡丹花式洗
　　高3.7公分　口徑11.6公分　足徑9.0公分
　　闕四三〇 52
Floral-shaped basin
Chiao-t'an-hsia Kuan ware,
Southern Sung Dynasty, 1127-1278
Height: 3.7cm
Diameter: mouth 11.6cm, base 9.0cm

139. 南宋　郊壇下官窯粉青牡丹花式洗
　　　高3.2公分　口徑12.0公分　足徑9.5公分
　　　崑二二六6
　　　Floral-shaped basin
　　　Chiao-t'an-hsia Kuan ware,
　　　Southern Sung Dynasty, 1127-1278
　　　Height: 3.2cm
　　　Diameter: mouth 12.0cm, base 9.5cm

140. 南宋　脩內司官窯淺青牡丹花式洗
　　　高3.4公分　口徑11.2公分　足徑8.4公分
　　　闕四二九66之2
Floral-shaped basin
Hsiu-nei-ssu Kuan ware,
Southern Sung Dynasty, 1127-1278
Height: 3.4cm
Diameter: mouth 11.2cm, base 8.4cm

141. 南宋　郊壇下官窯灰青牡丹花式洗
　　 高3.5公分　口徑11.0×11.5公分
　　 底徑8.7×8.6公分　崑二二八 65
　　 Floral-shaped basin
　　 Chiao-t'an-hsia Kuan ware,
　　 Southern Sung Dynasty, 1127-1278
　　 Height: 3.5cm
　　 Mouth dimensions: 11.5 x 11.0cm
　　 Base dimensions: 8.7 x 8.6cm

142. 南宋　郊壇下官窯灰青牡丹花式洗
　　　高3.0公分　口徑11.7公分　底徑8.3公分
　　　JW92
　　　Floral-shaped basin
　　　Chiao-t'an-hsia Kuan ware,
　　　Southern Sung Dynasty, 1127-1278
　　　Height: 3.0cm
　　　Diameter: mouth 11.7cm, base 8.3cm

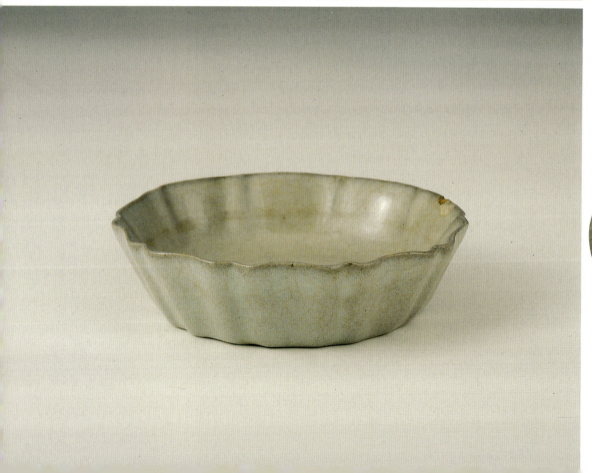

143. 南宋　脩內司官窯粉青牡丹花式洗
　　　高1.2公分　口徑15.8公分　足徑6.3公分
　　　麗一一二九 3之6
　　　Floral-shaped basin
　　　Hsiu-nei-ssu Kuan ware,
　　　Southern Sung Dynasty, 1127-1278
　　　Height: 1.2cm
　　　Diameter: mouth 15.8cm, base 6.3cm

統一編號
020018780184

版權所有

中華民國七十八年十月初版一刷
中華民國 八 十 年八月初版二刷
中華民國八十五年二月初版三刷

中華民國新聞局登記證局版臺業字第2621號

# 宋官窯特展

發行人：秦　　　孝　　　儀
編輯者：國立故宮博物院編輯委員會
出版者：國 立 故 宮 博 物 院
　　　　中華民國台北市士林區外雙溪
　　　　電話：(02) 8 8 1 2 0 2 1 ─ 4
　　　　電傳：(02) 8 8 2 ─ 1 4 4 0
　　　　劃撥帳號：0012874─1
印刷者：裕 台 公 司 中 華 印 刷 廠
　　　　台 北 縣 新 店 市 寶 強 路 6 號
　　　　電 話 ：(02) 9 1 1 0 1 1 1 ─ 6

Copyright © 1989 by the National Palace Museum

First Printing , October 1989
Second Printing , August 1991
Third Printing , February 1996

**CATALOGUE OF THE SPECIAL EXHIBITION
OF SUNG DYNASTY KUAN WARE**

DIRECTOR : Chin Hsiao-i
PUBLISHER : NATIONAL PALACE MUSEUM
　　　　　　Wai-shuang-hsi, Shih-lin, Taipei 111, Taiwan,
　　　　　　Republic of China
　　　　　　TEL: 886-2-8812021 , FAX: 886-2-8821440
PRINTER : China Art Printing Works Yu-Tai Industrial Corp., Ltd.
　　　　　　6 , Pao-chiang Road, Hsintien 231, Taipei Taiwan,
　　　　　　Republic of China
　　　　　　TEL: 886-2-9110111 , FAX: 886-2-9189578
ISBN 957-562-073-9